Numbers & alphabets

 Book

This Book Belongs to the Owesome Kid :

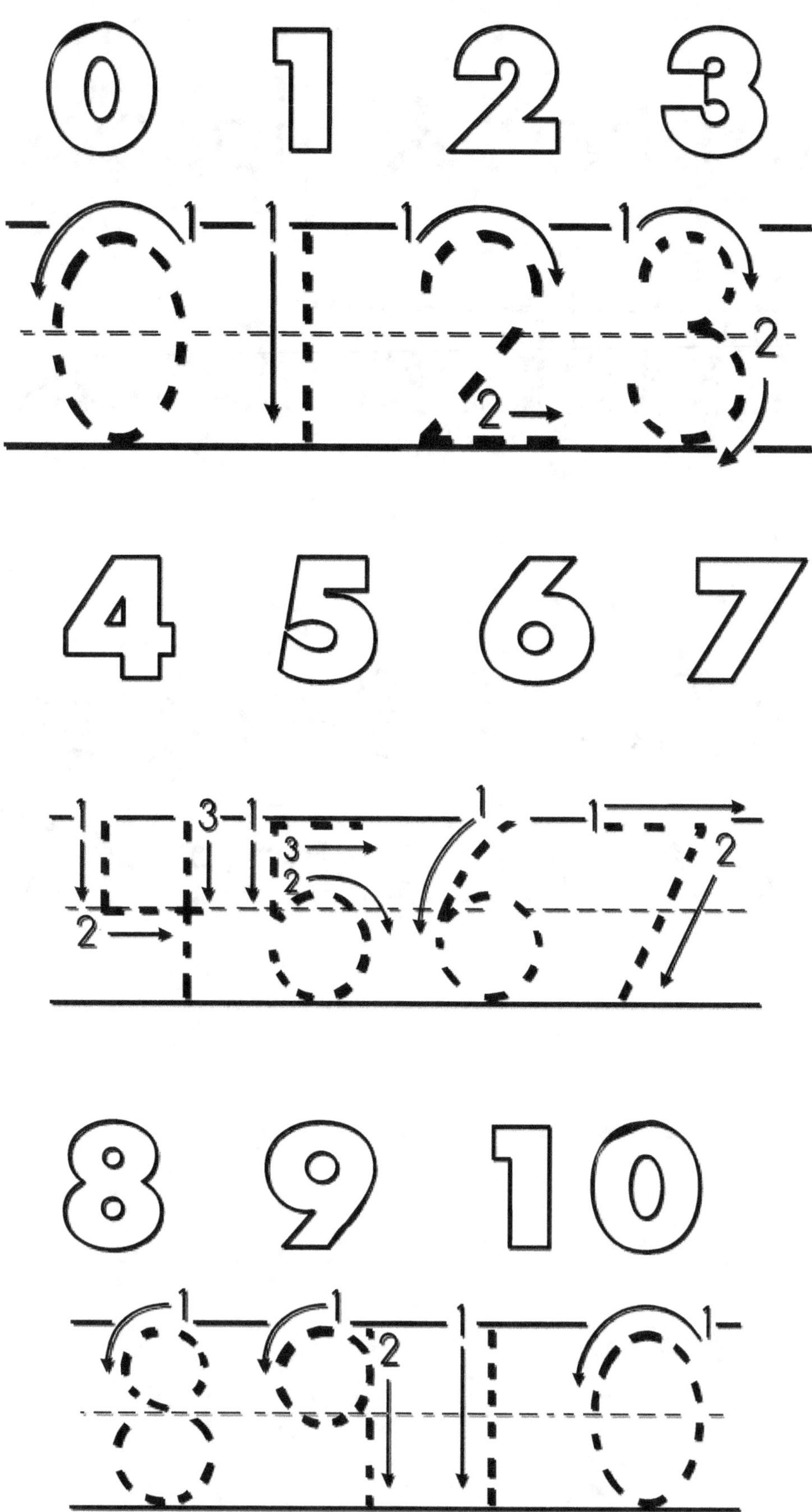

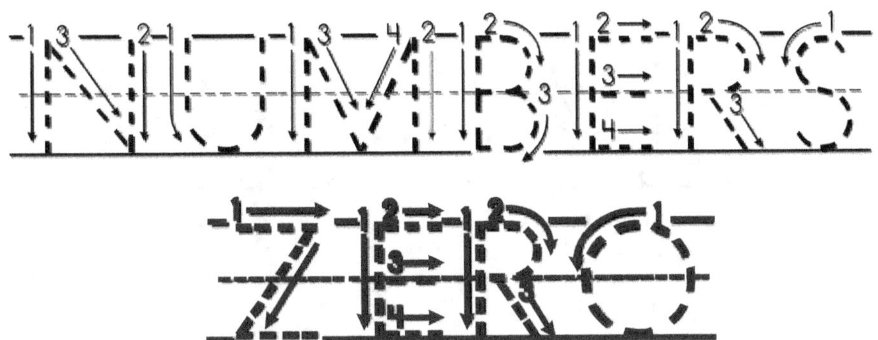

NUMBERS
ZERO

trace and copy the numbers

0

0   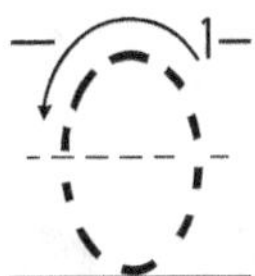 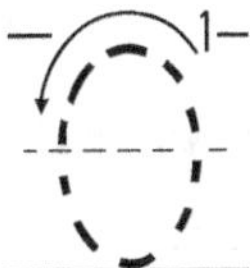 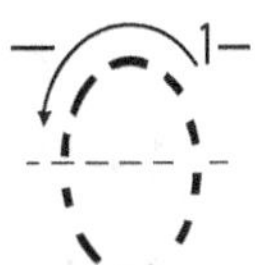 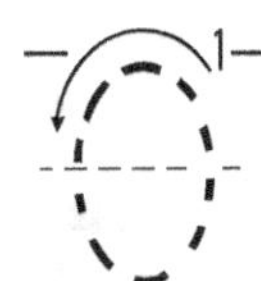

0    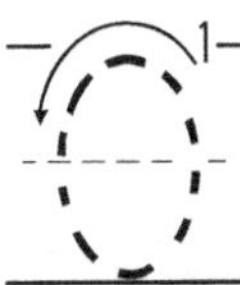 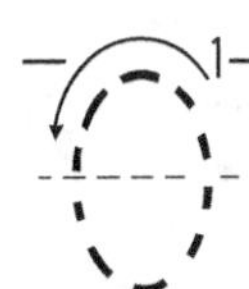 

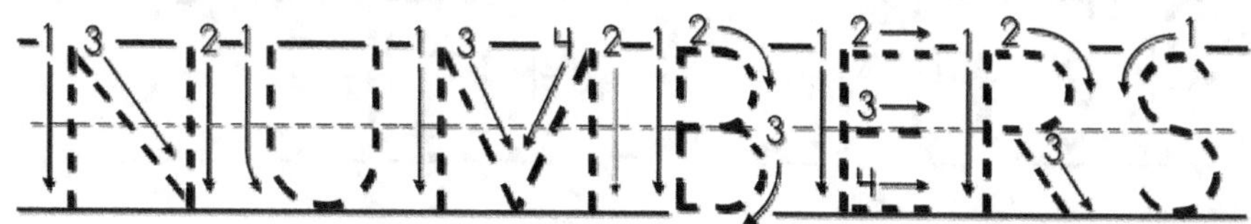

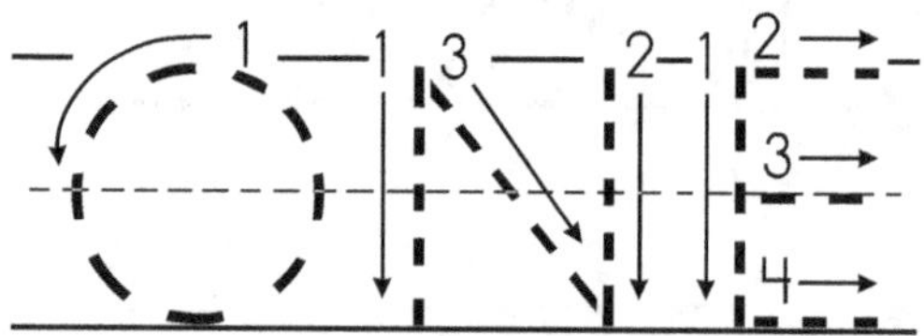

trace and copy the numbers

1 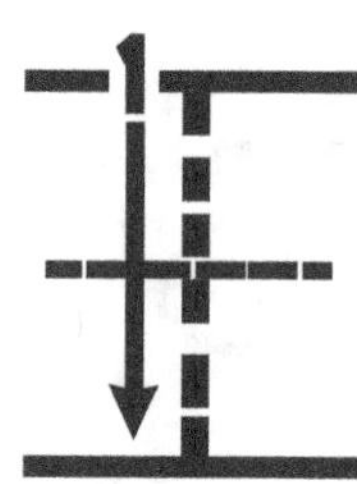 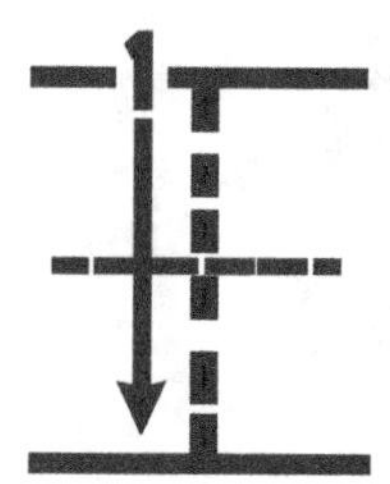

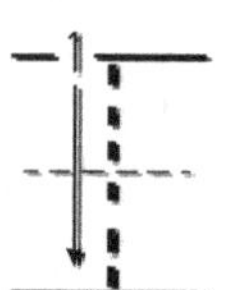

1

1

trace and copy the numbers

2  

2    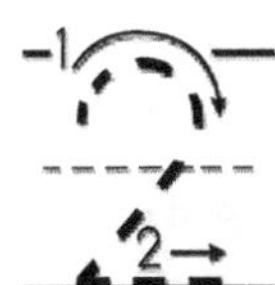

2   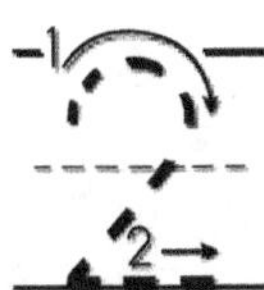 

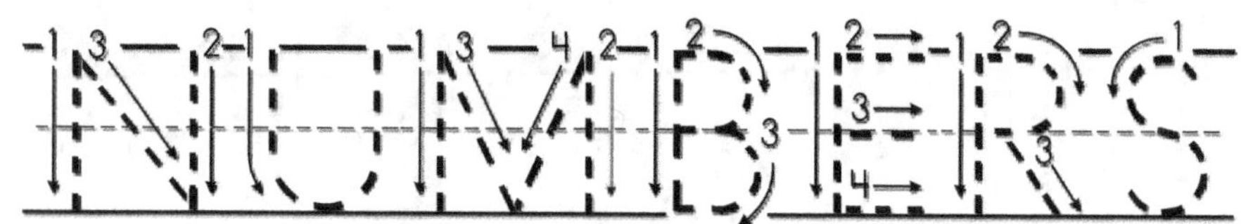

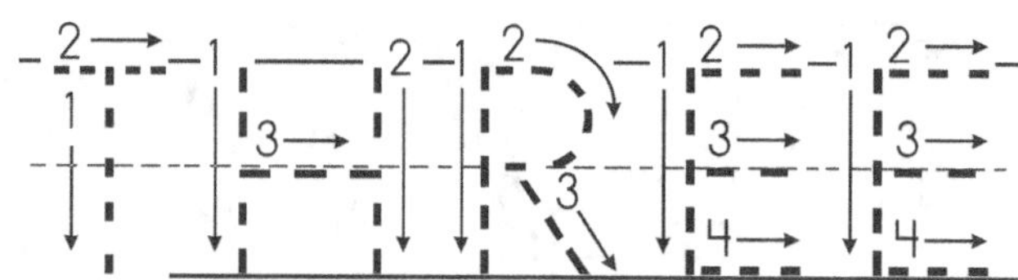

trace and copy the numbers

3  

THREE

3    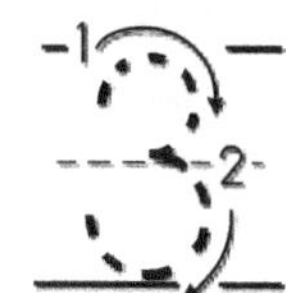

3  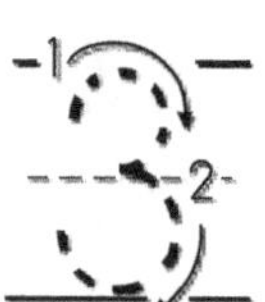 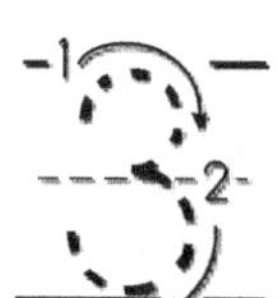 

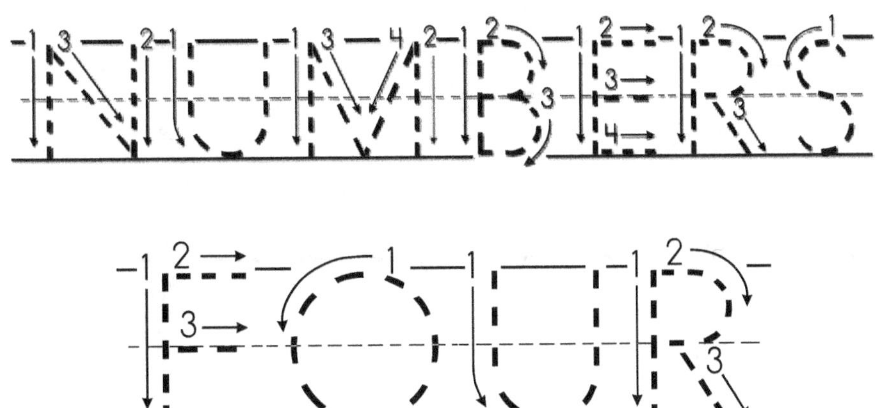

trace and copy the numbers

4 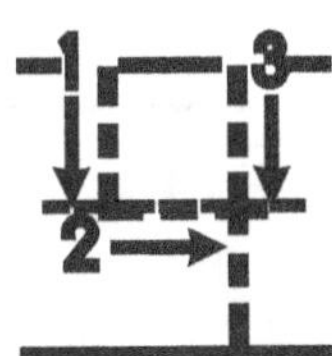 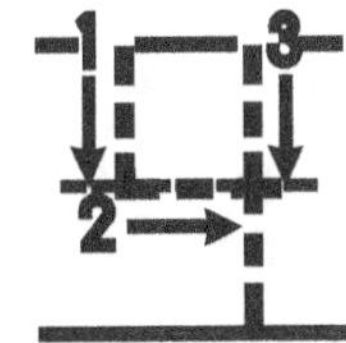

FOUR

4 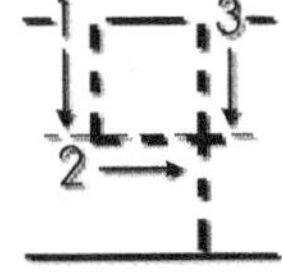 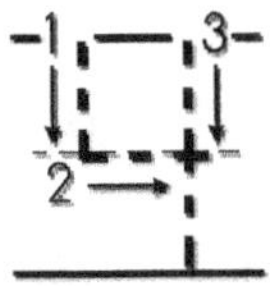 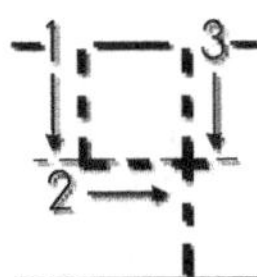 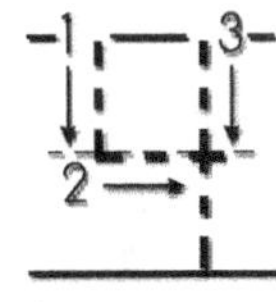

4 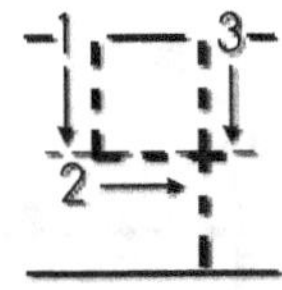 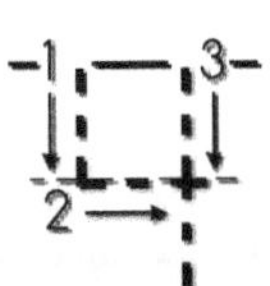

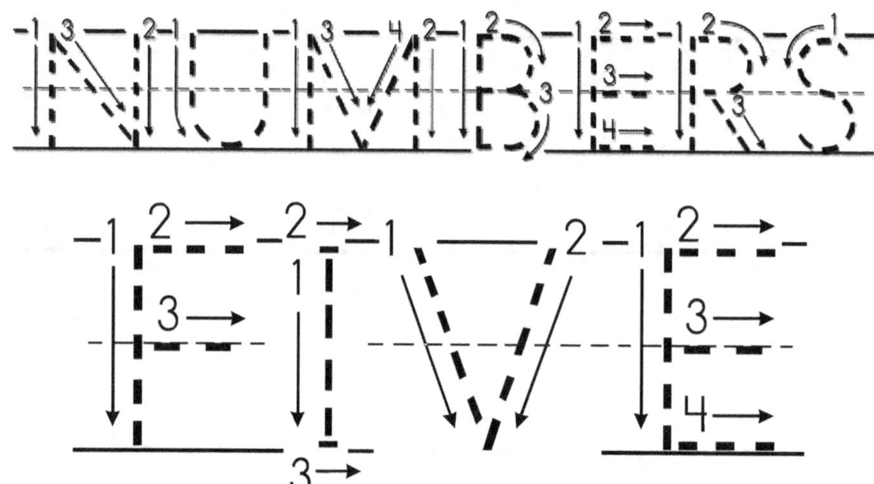

trace and copy the numbers

5  

5 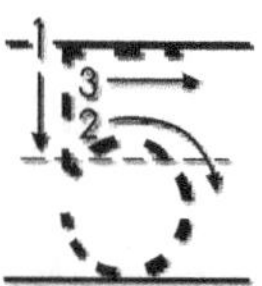  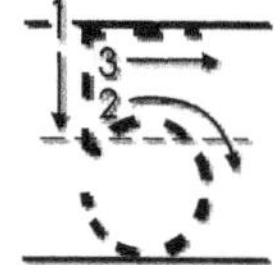 

5    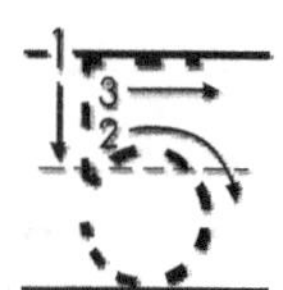

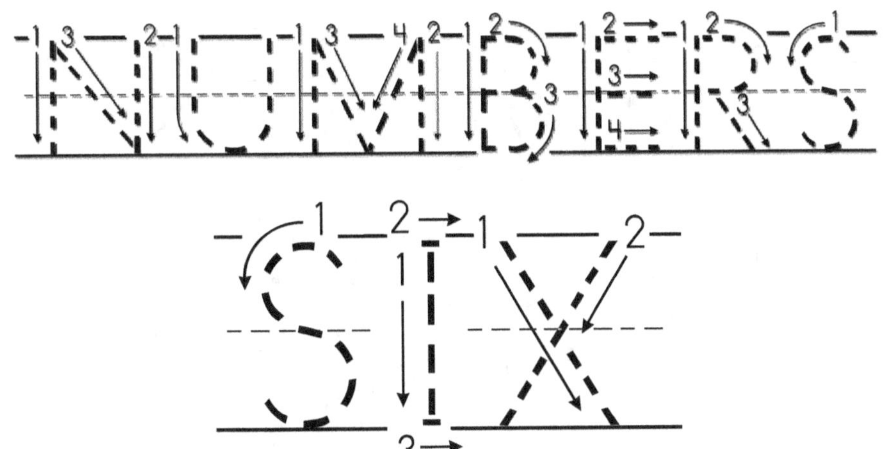

trace and copy the numbers

6  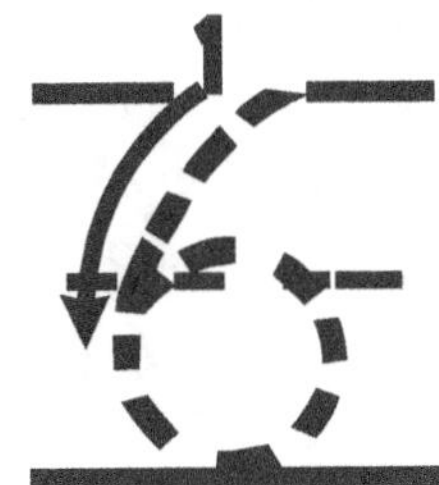 

6  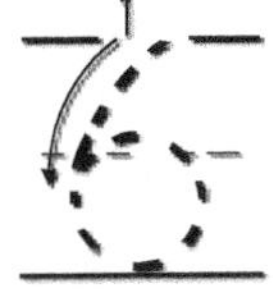 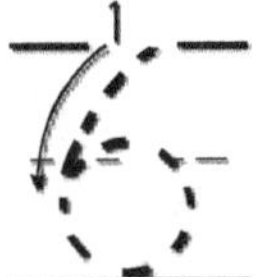  

6 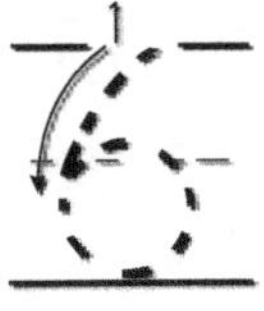 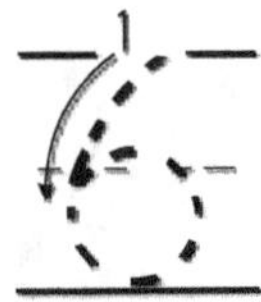  

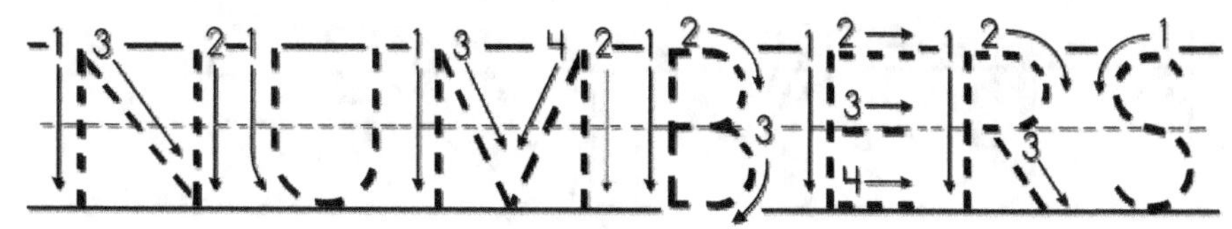

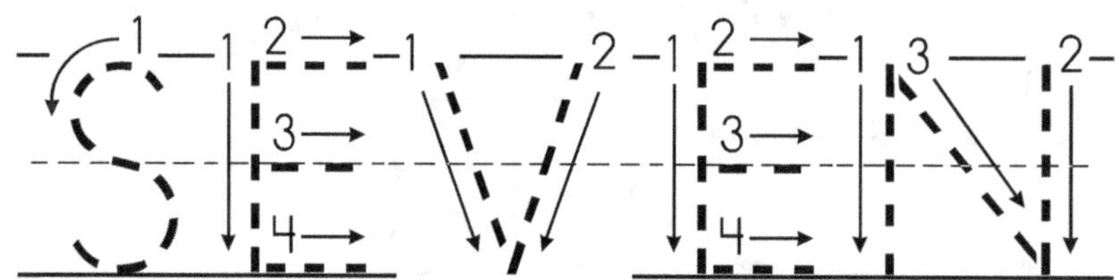

trace and copy the numbers

7 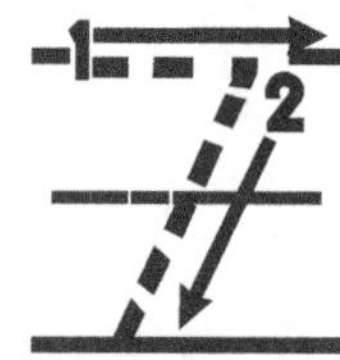 

7

7

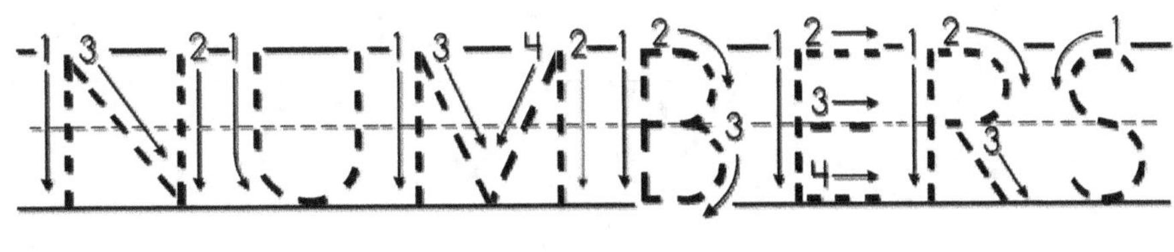

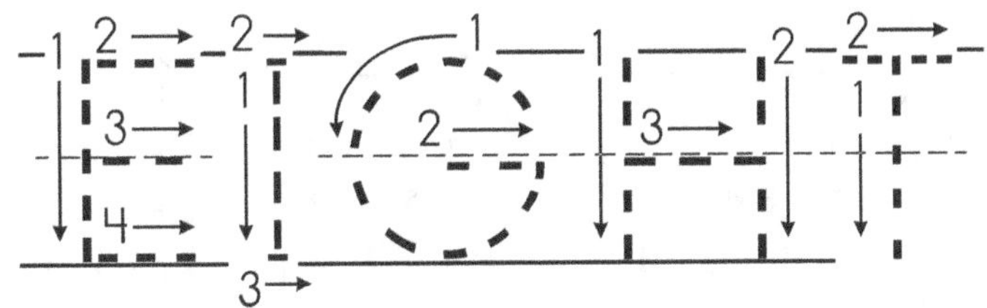

trace and copy the numbers

8  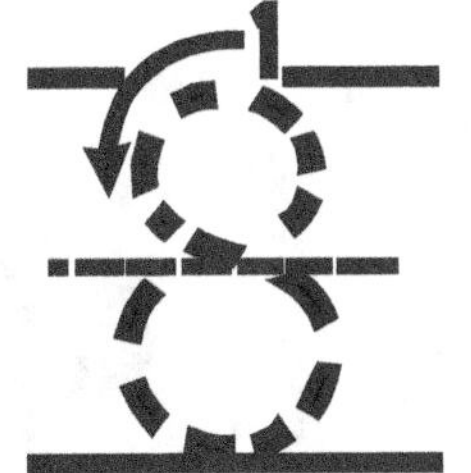

8 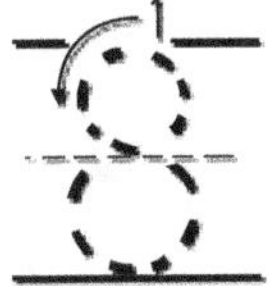 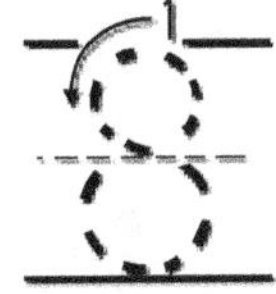 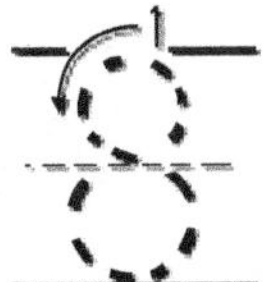 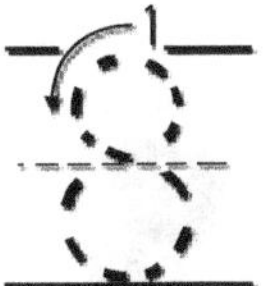

8 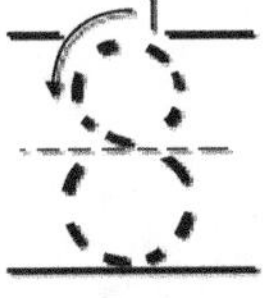 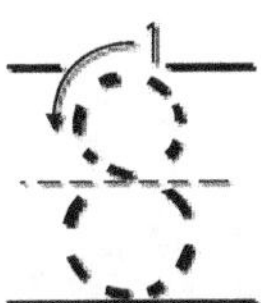 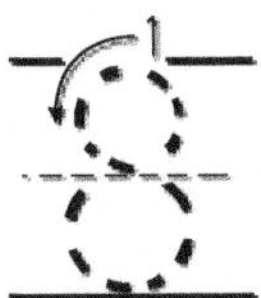 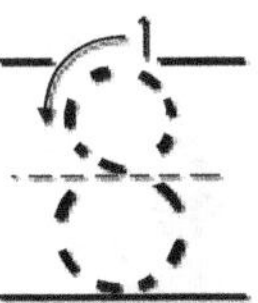

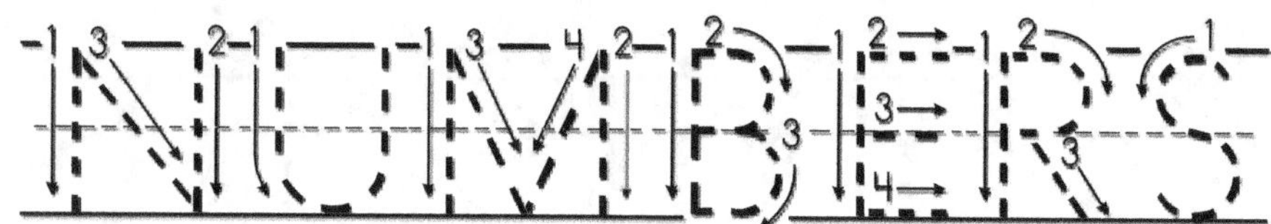

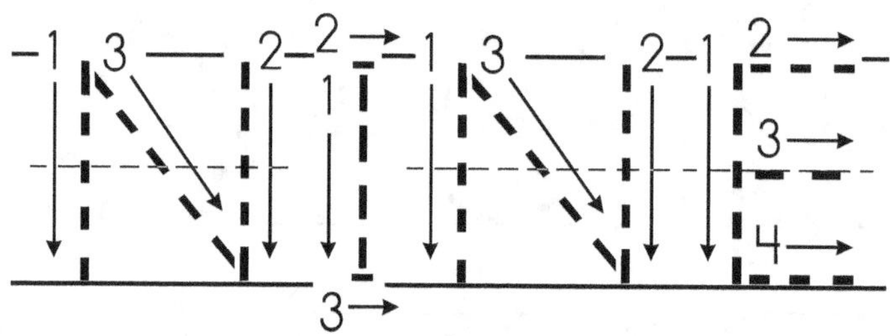

trace and copy the numbers

9 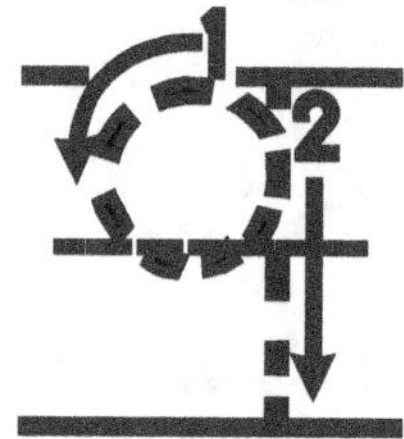 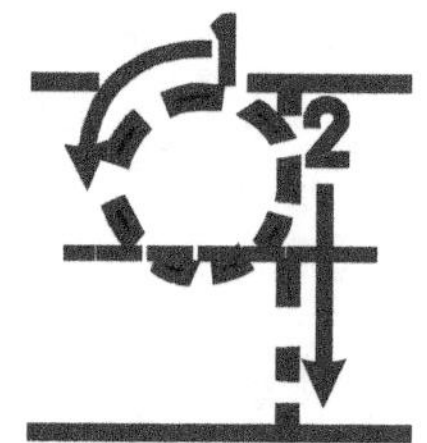

9 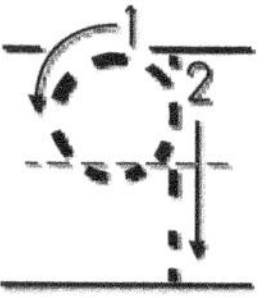 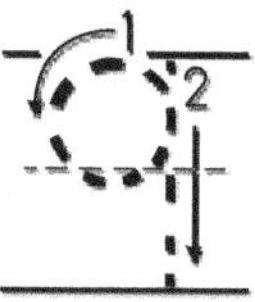 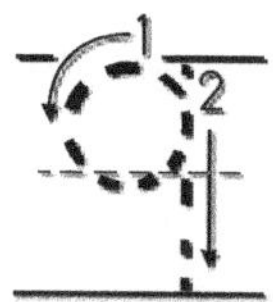 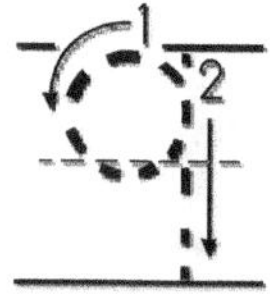

9 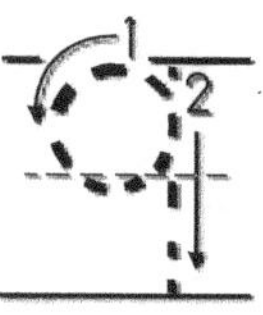   

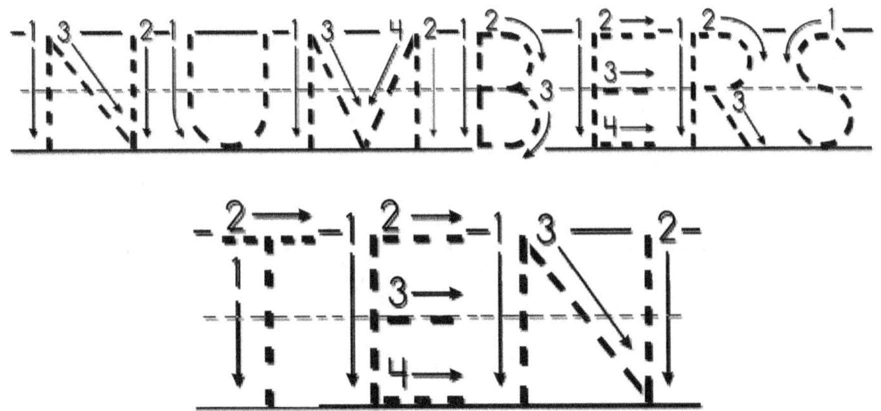

trace and copy the numbers

10  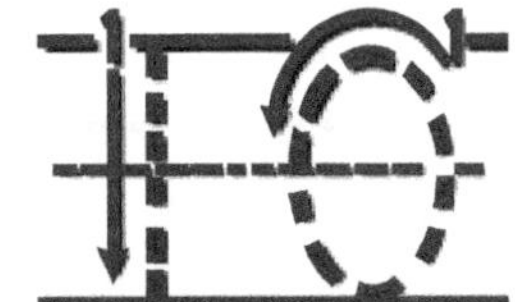

10 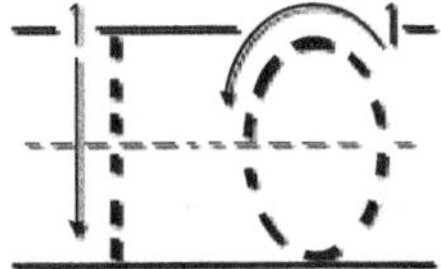  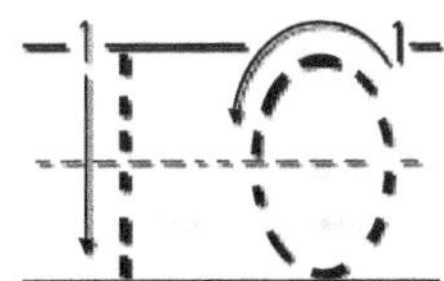

10 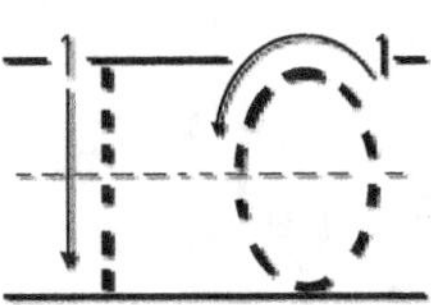  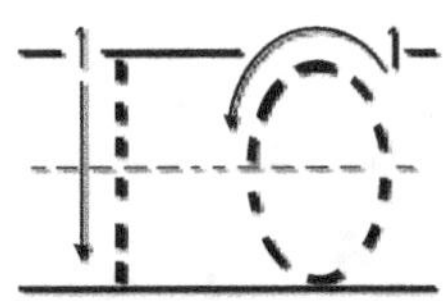

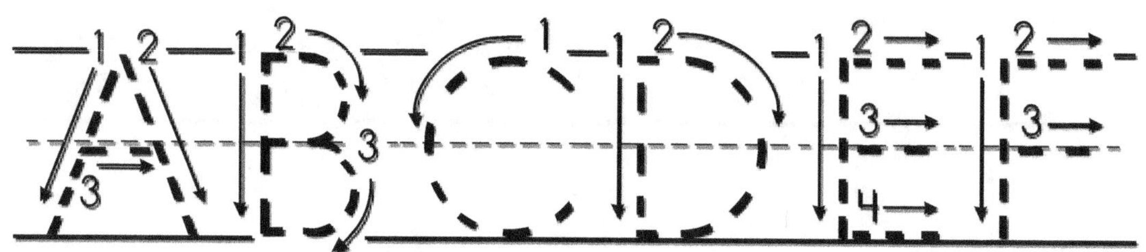

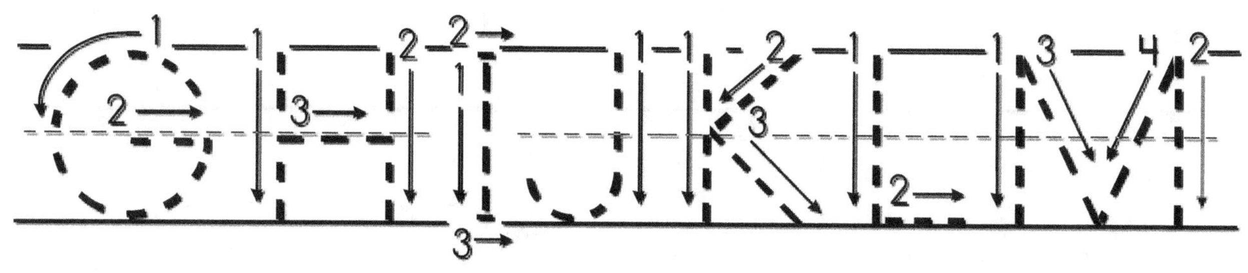

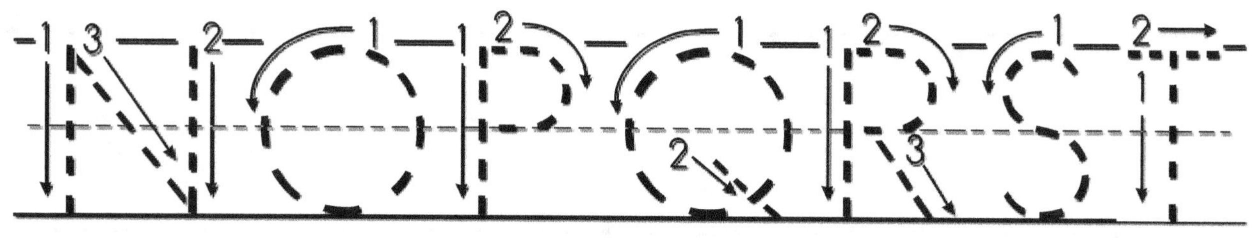

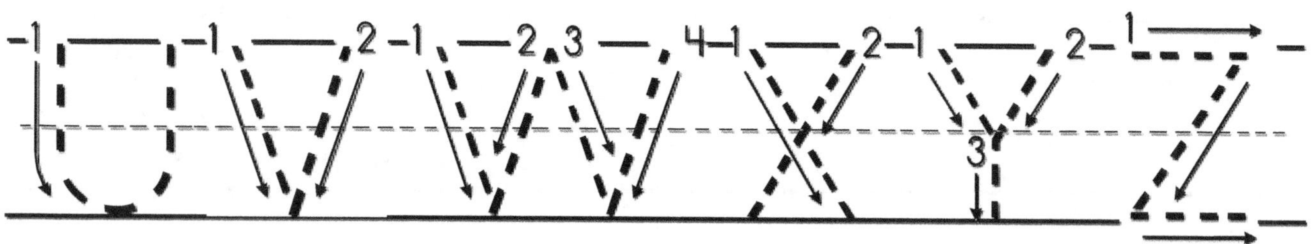

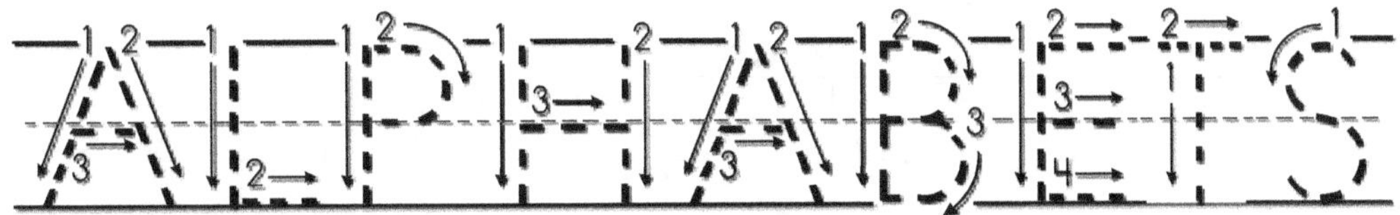

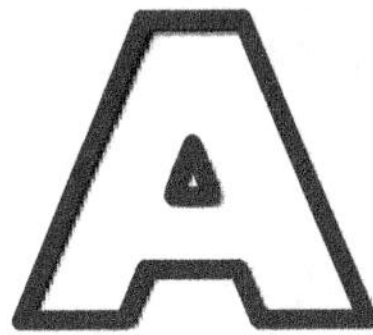

trace and copy the letters

A

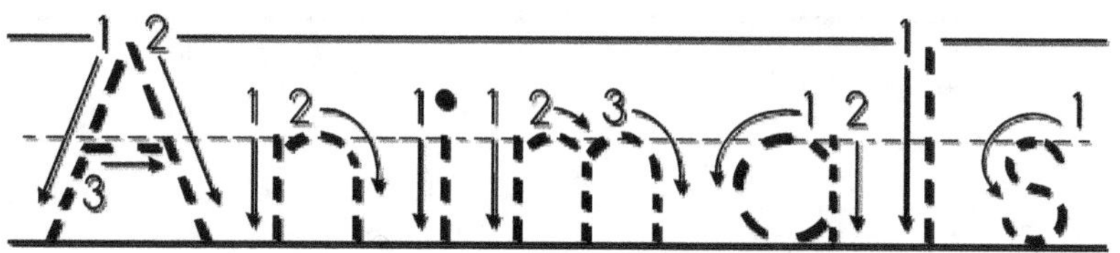

ALPHABETS

B

trace and copy the letters

B

b

b

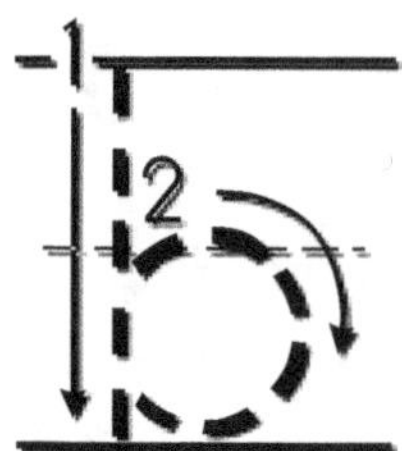

B

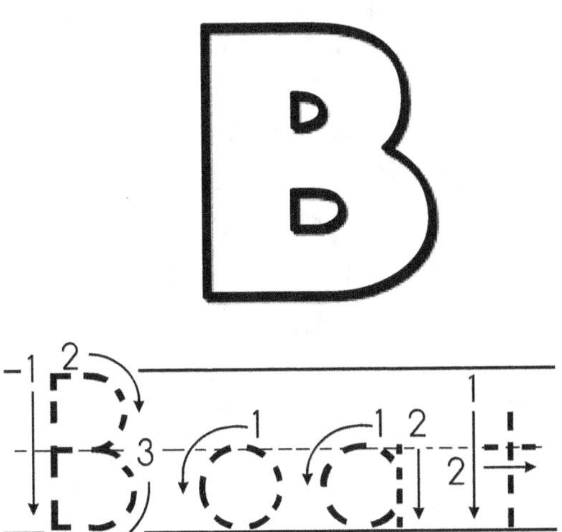

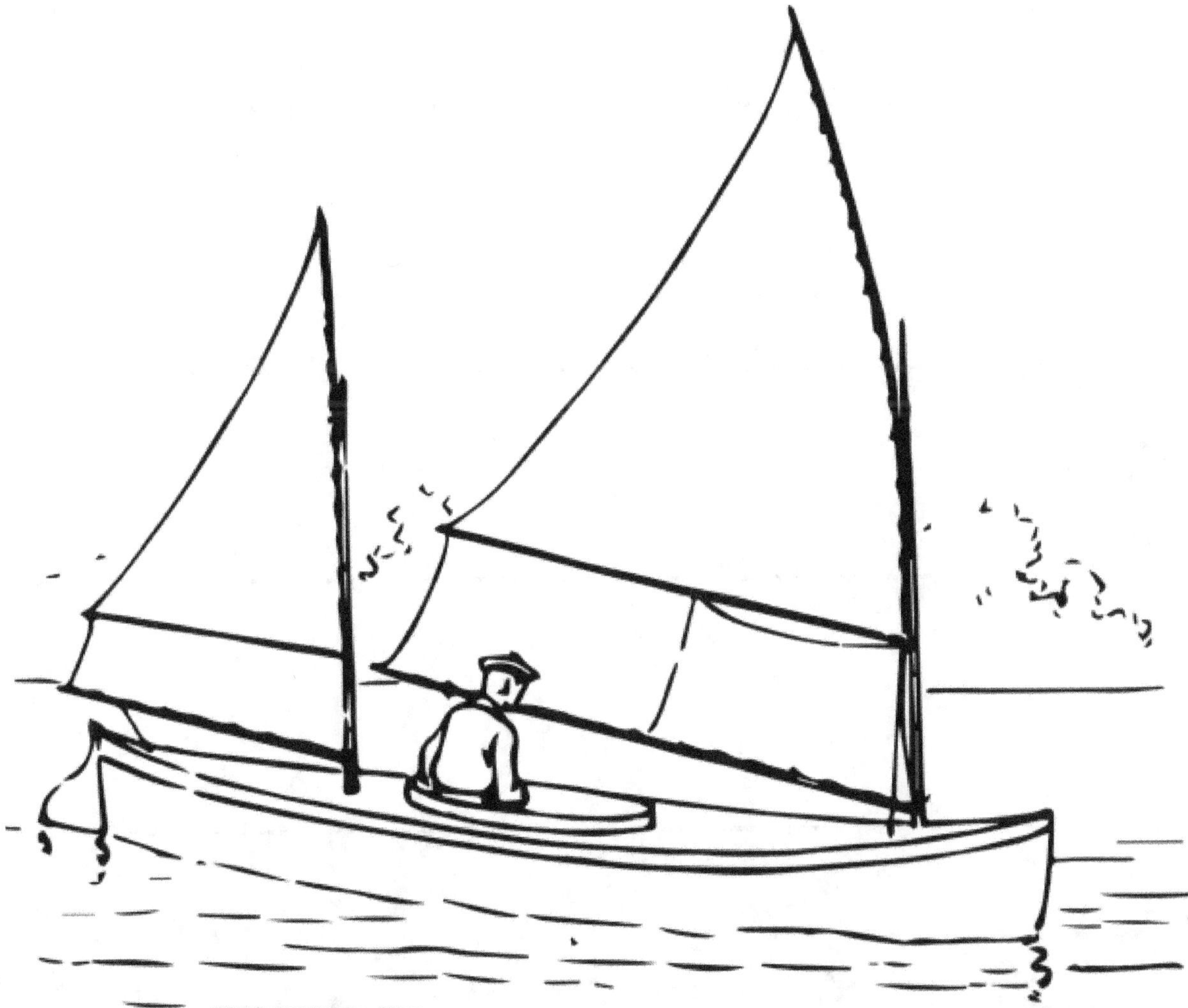

ALPHABETS
C
trace and copy the letters

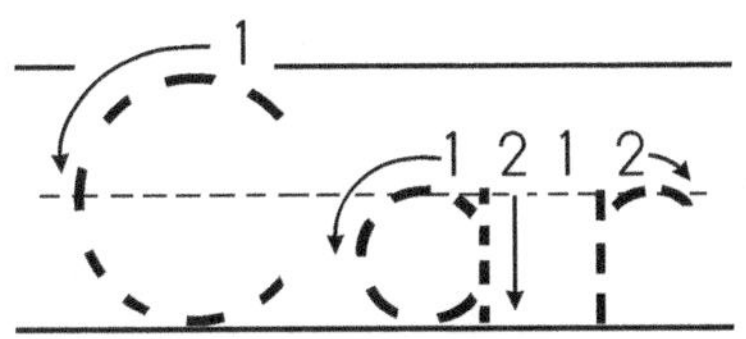
Car

ALPHABETS
D
trace and copy the letters

D

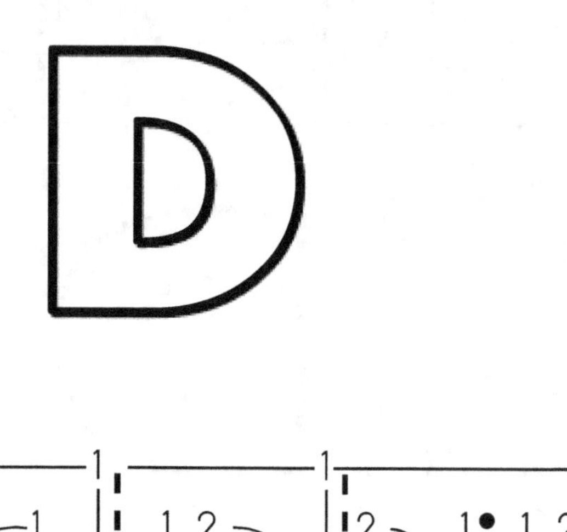

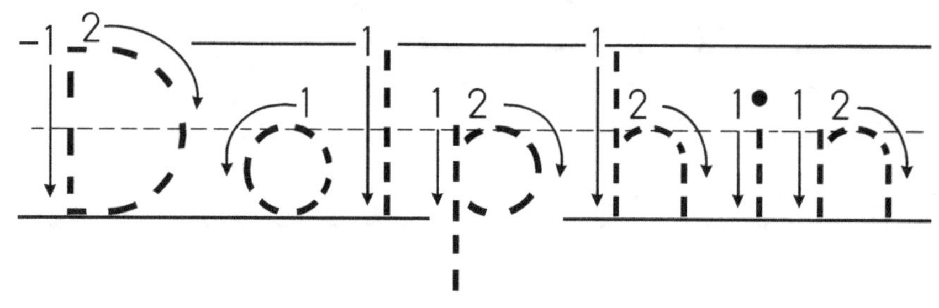

ALPHABETS
E
trace and copy the letters

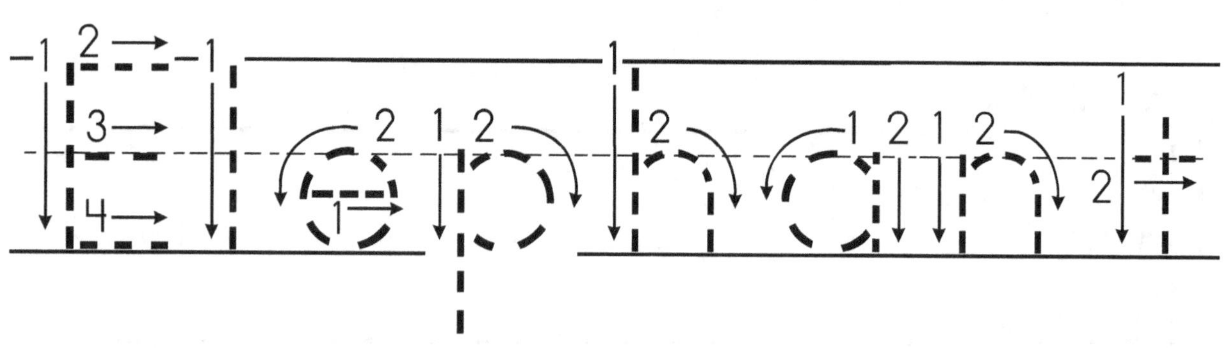
Elephant

ALPHABETS

F

trace and copy the letters

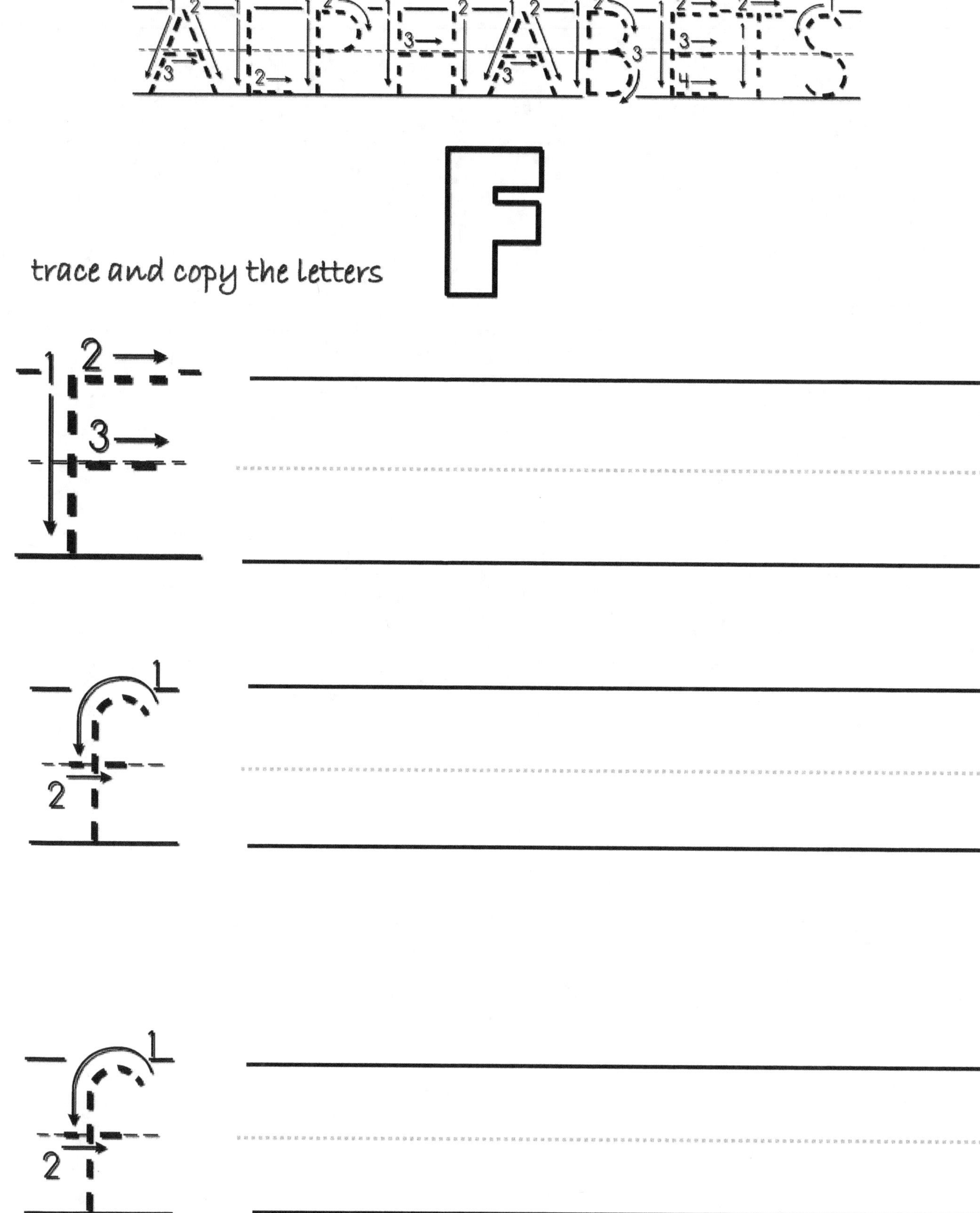

F

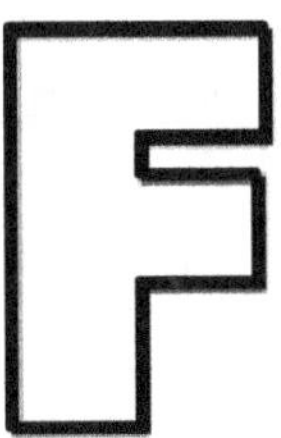

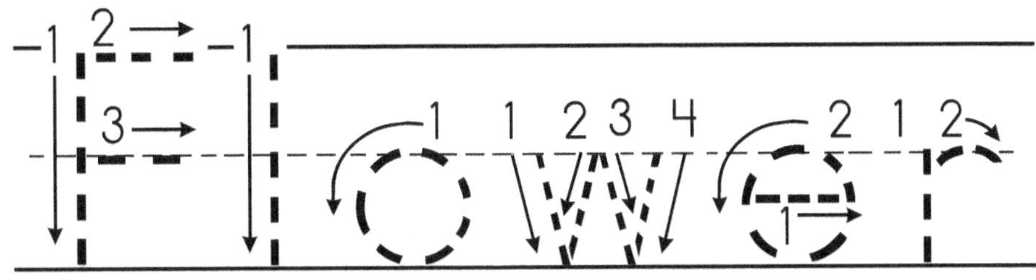

ALPHABETS

trace and copy the letters

G

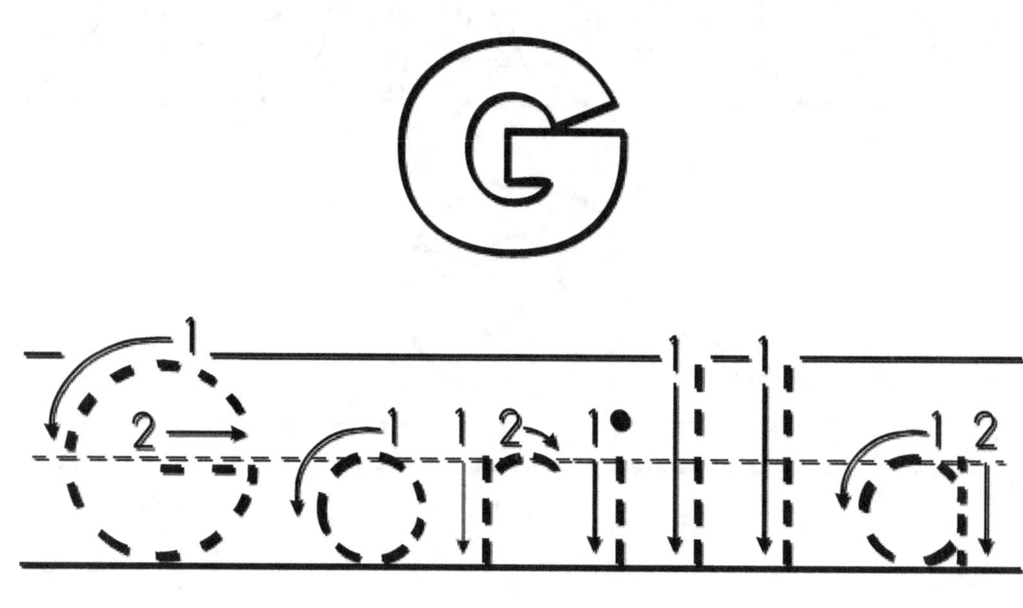

ALPHABETS

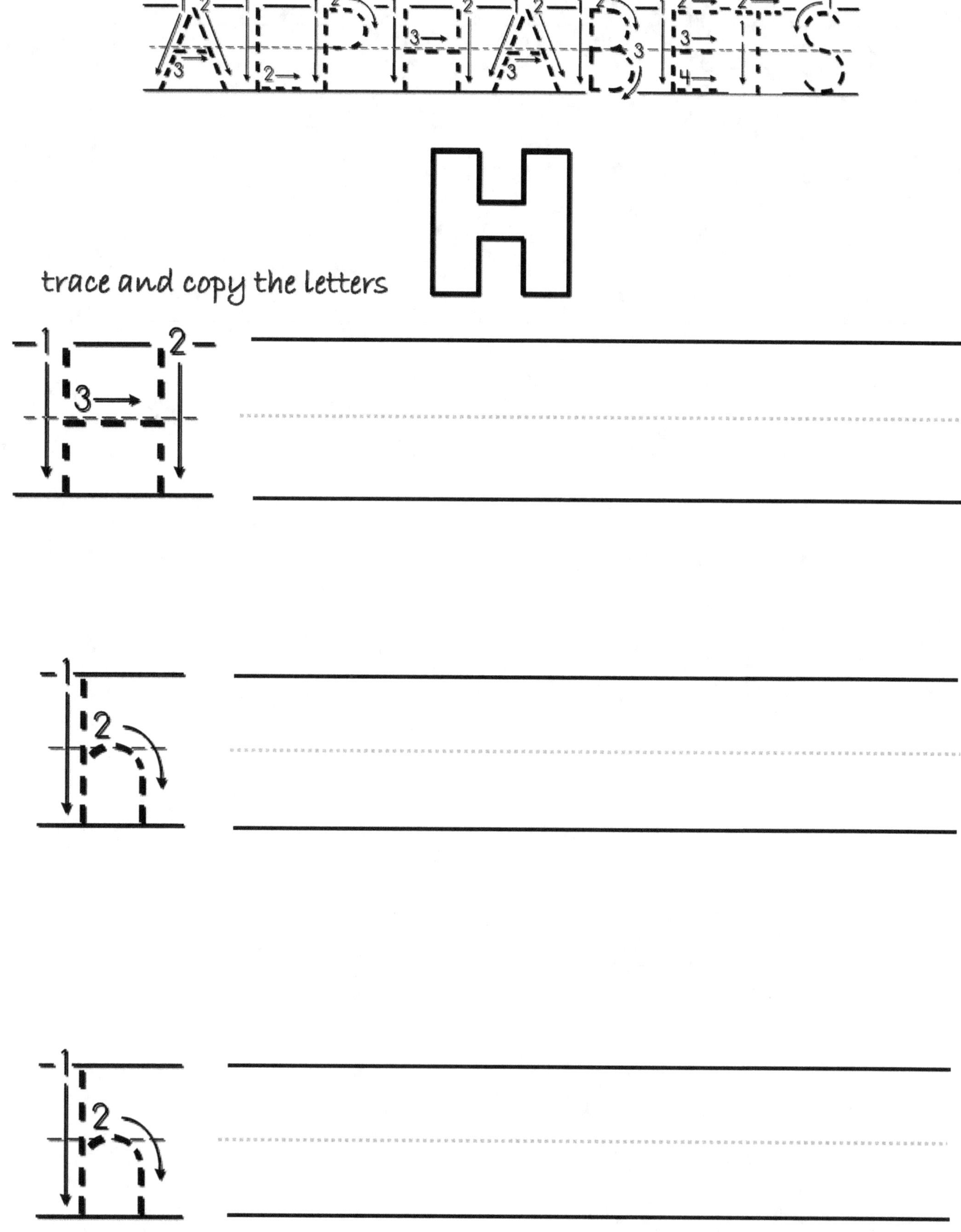

H

trace and copy the letters

H

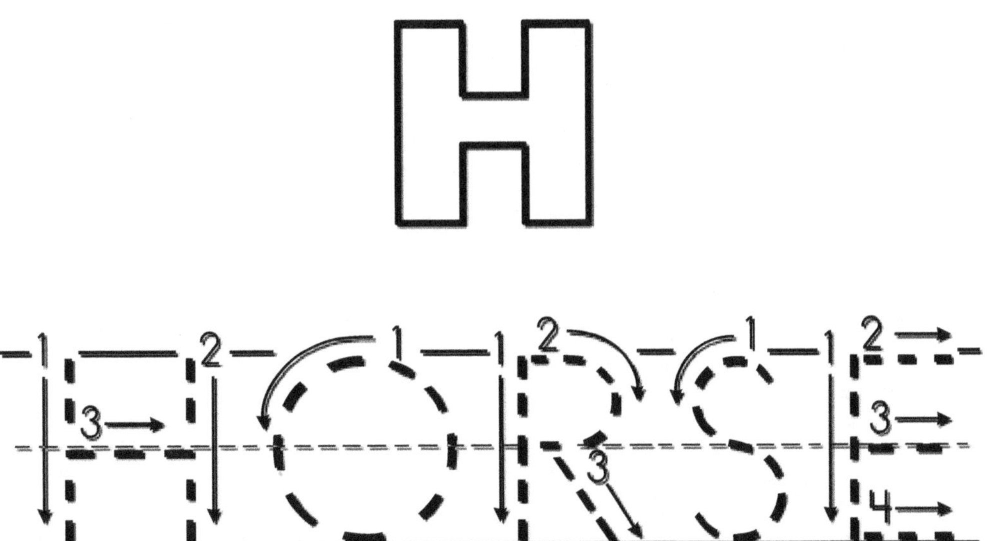

ALPHABETS

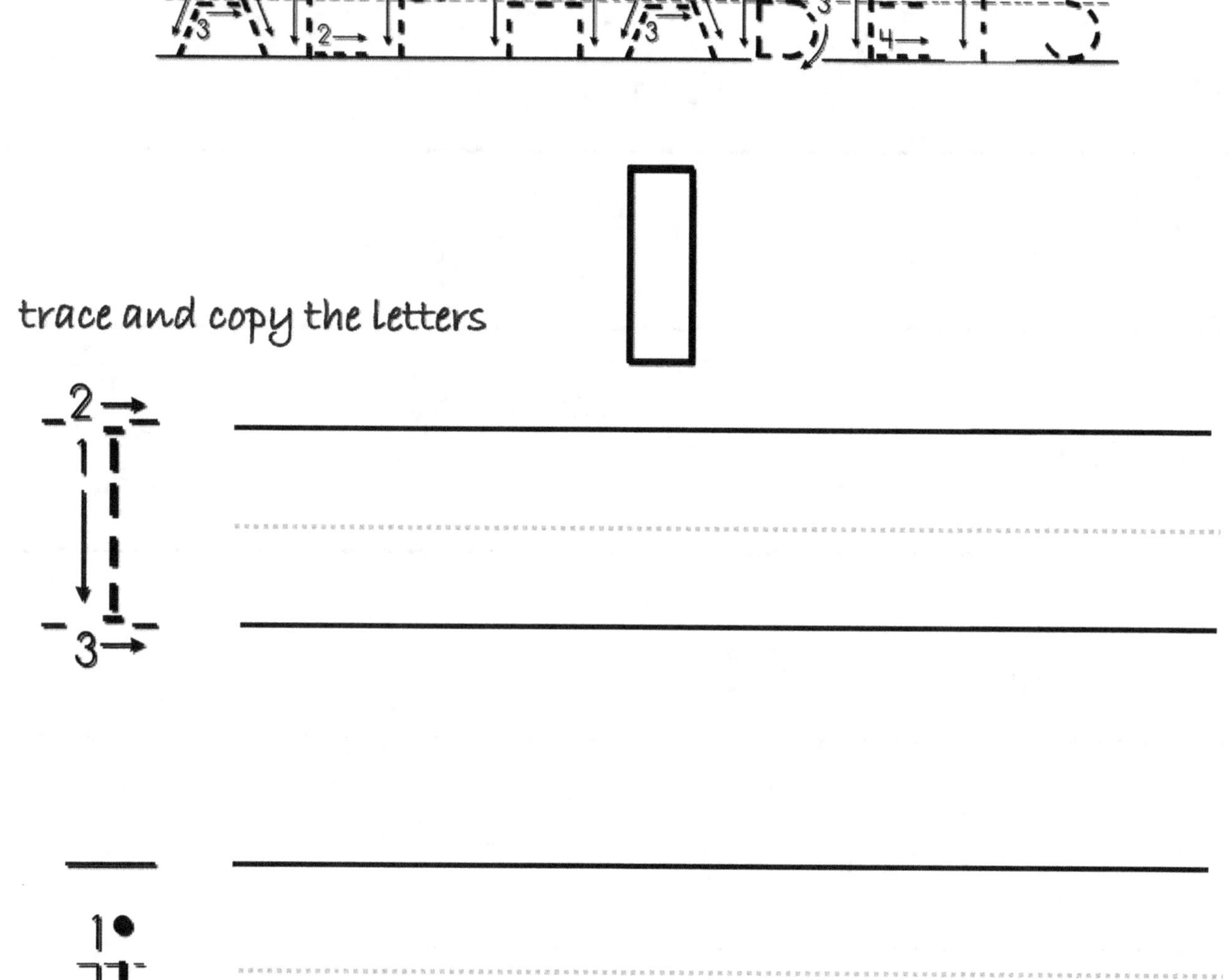

trace and copy the letters

I

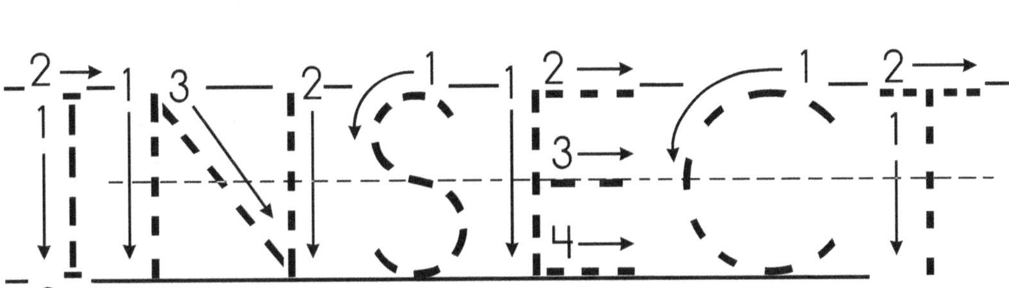

ALPHABETS

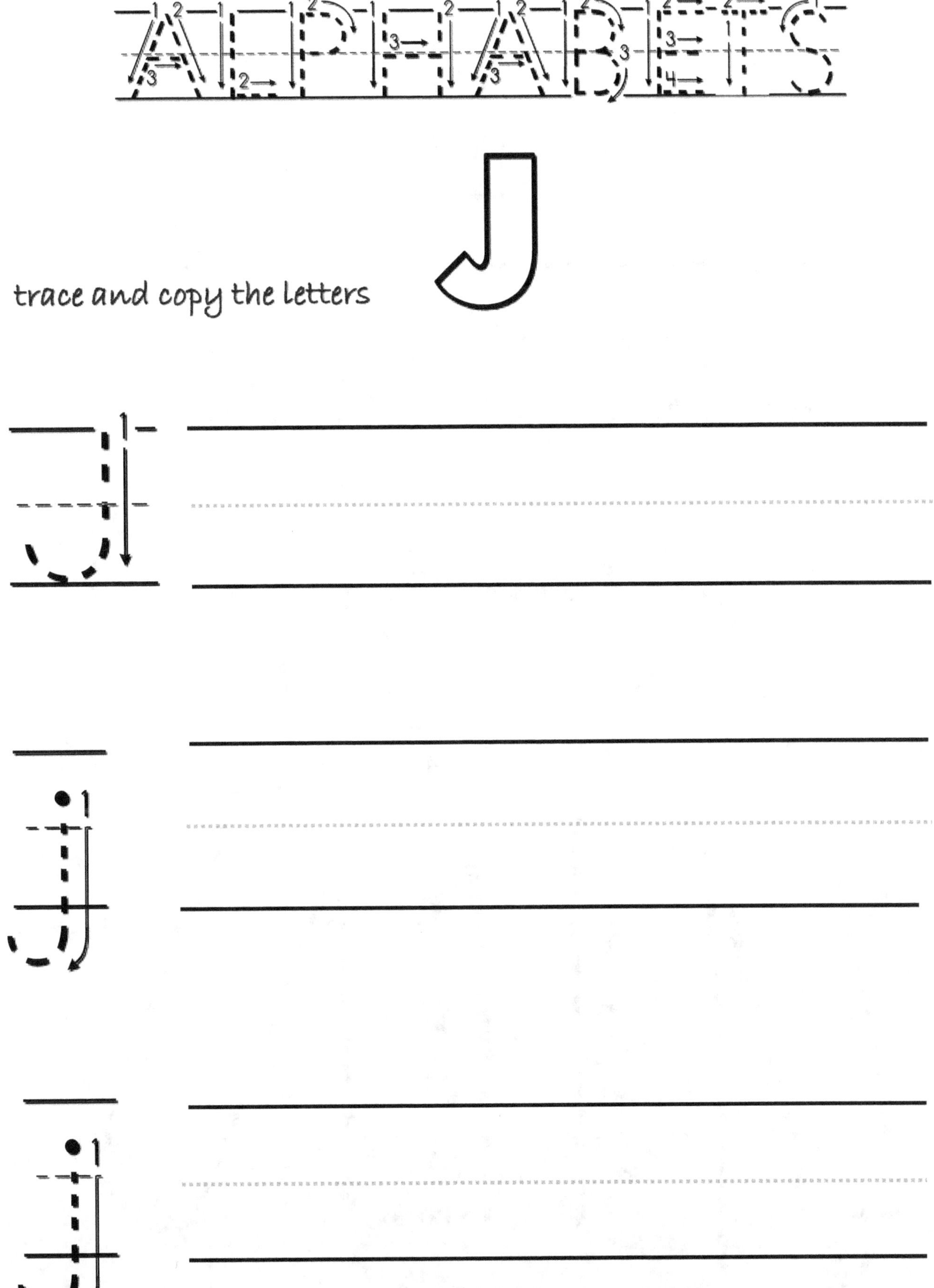

trace and copy the letters

J

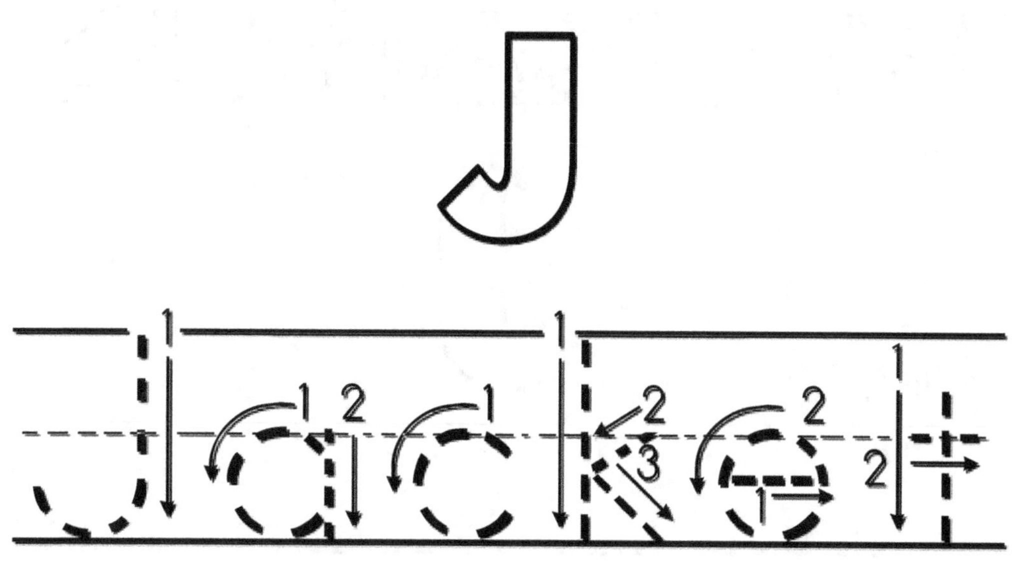

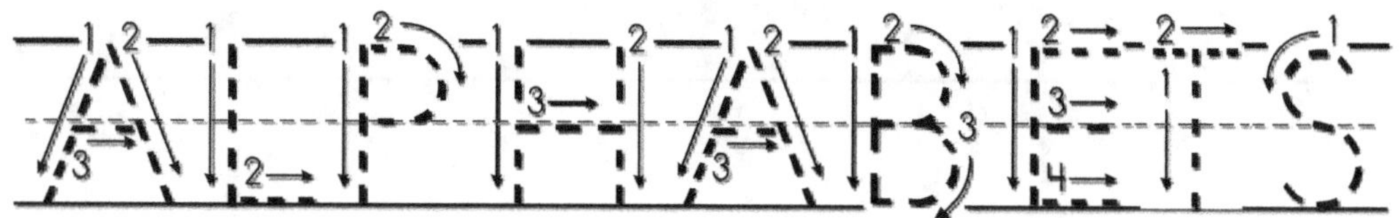

trace and copy the letters

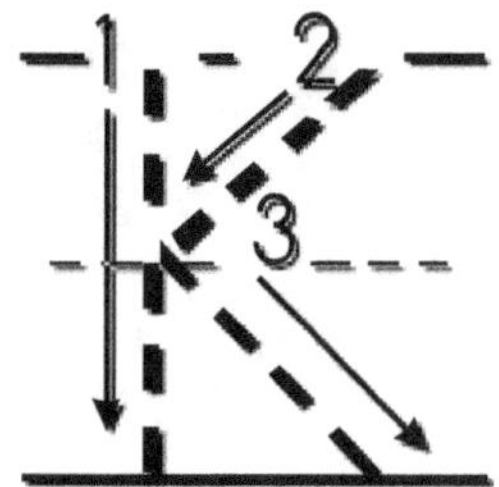

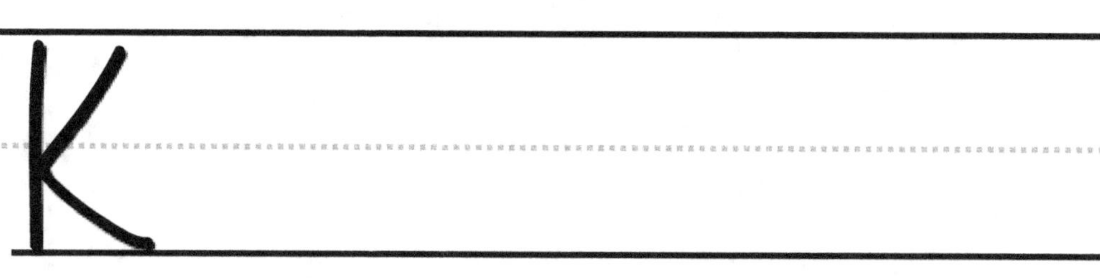

K

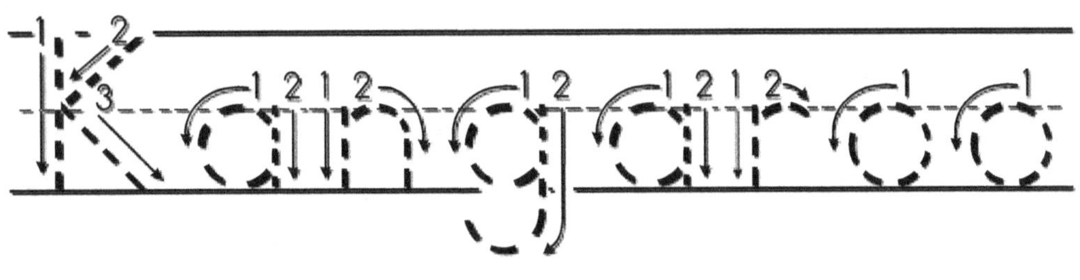

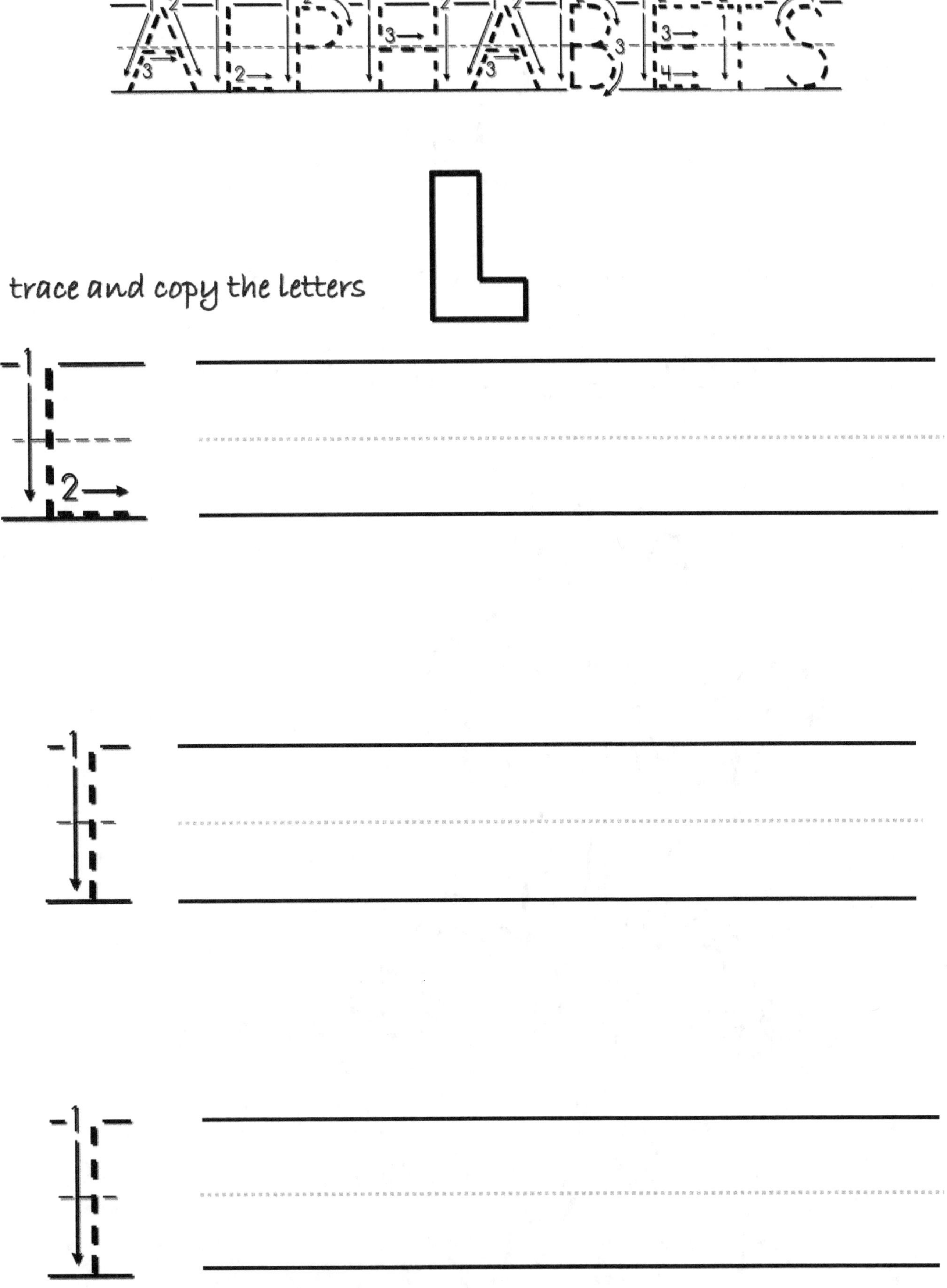

ALPHABETS
trace and copy the letters
L

L

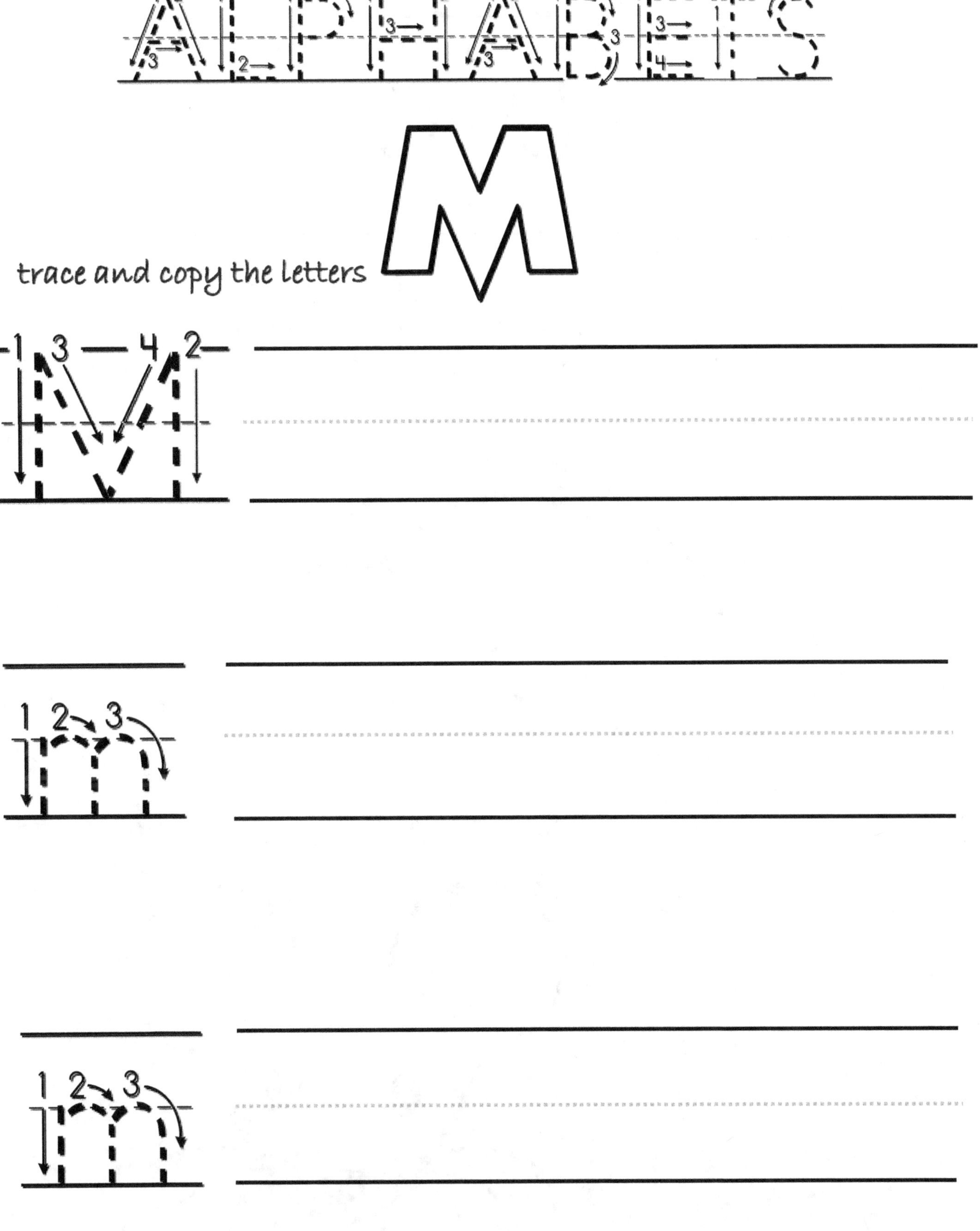

ALPHABETS
M
trace and copy the letters

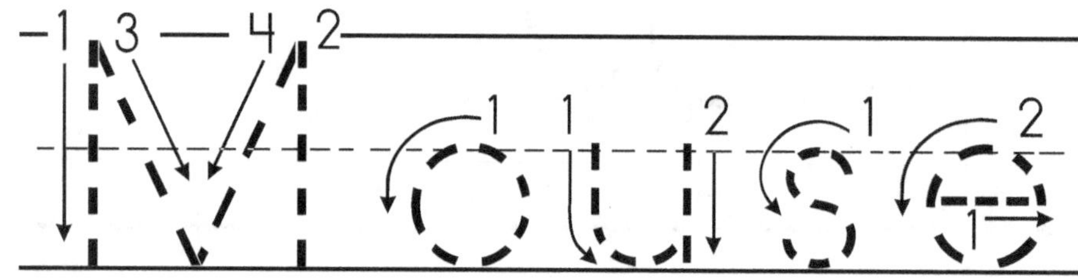

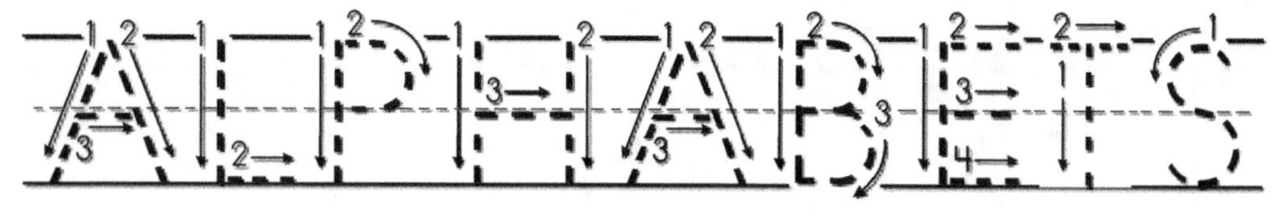

N

trace and copy the letters 

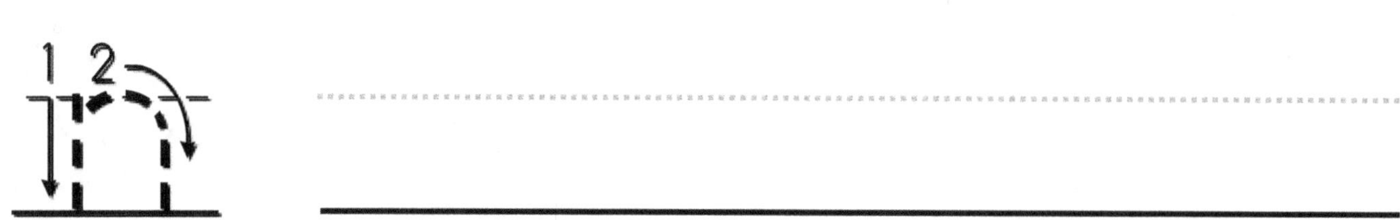

N

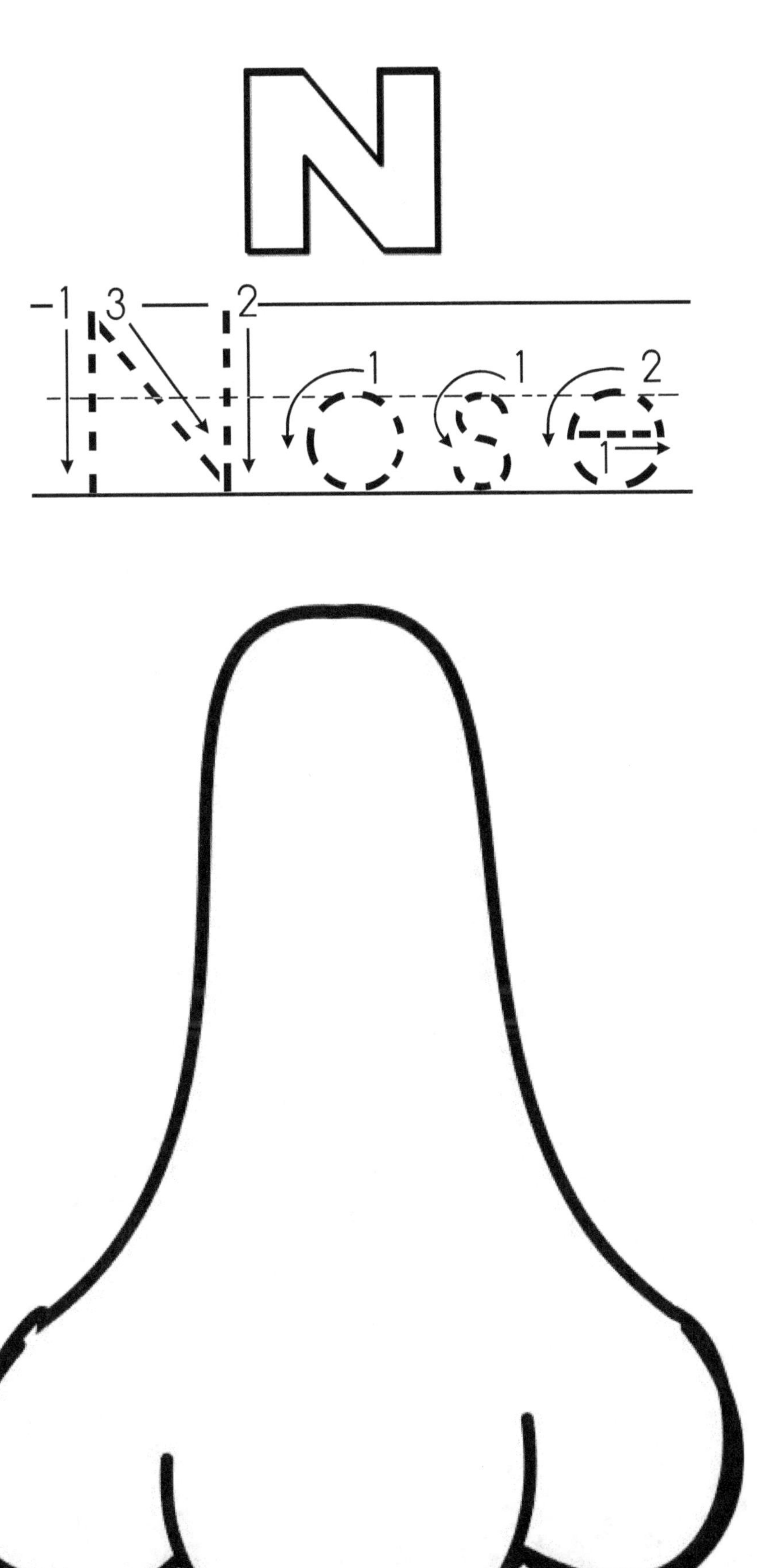

ALPHABETS

trace and copy the letters

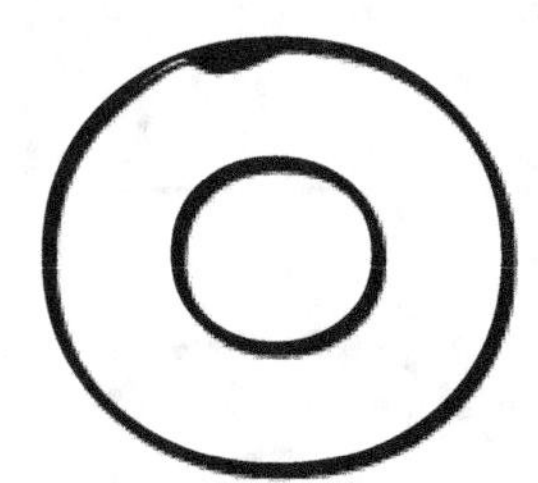

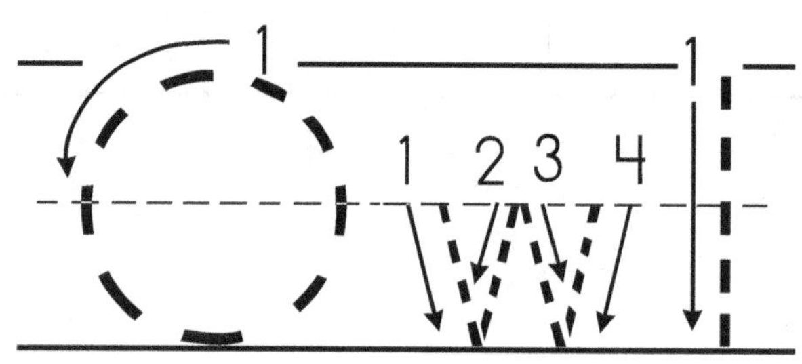

1
1
1 2 3 4
W

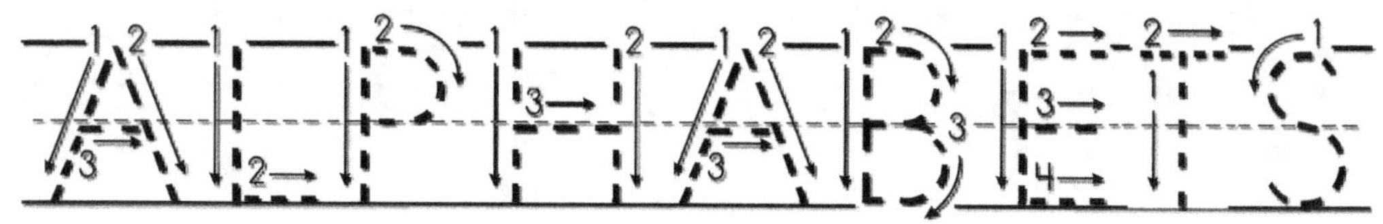

trace and copy the letters

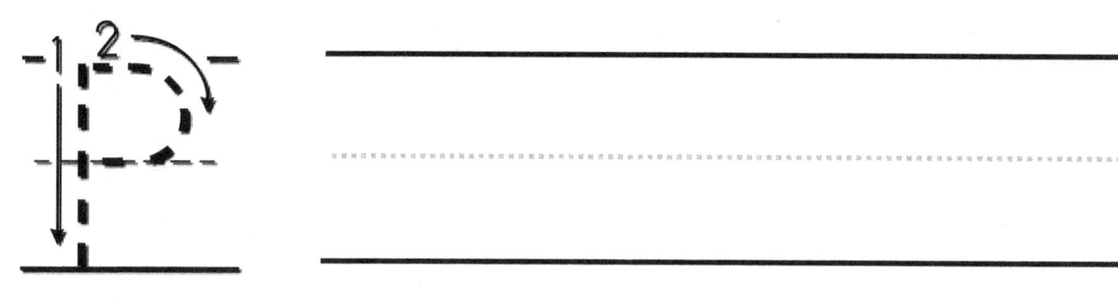

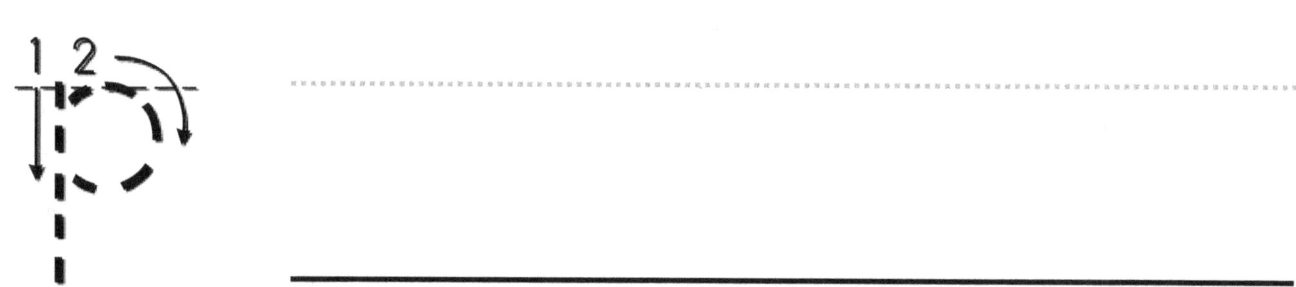

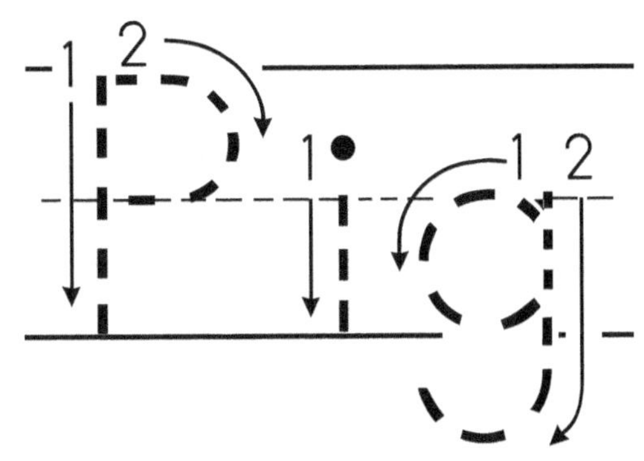

ALPHABETS

Q

trace and copy the letters

Q

q

q

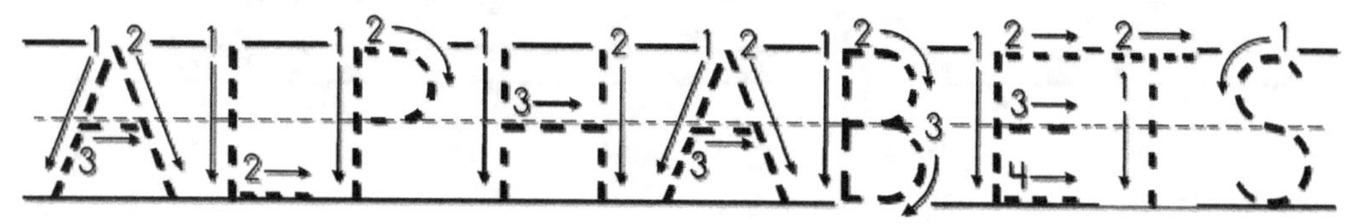

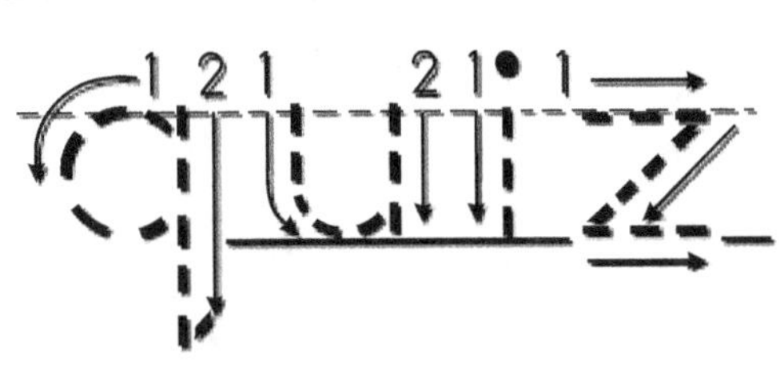

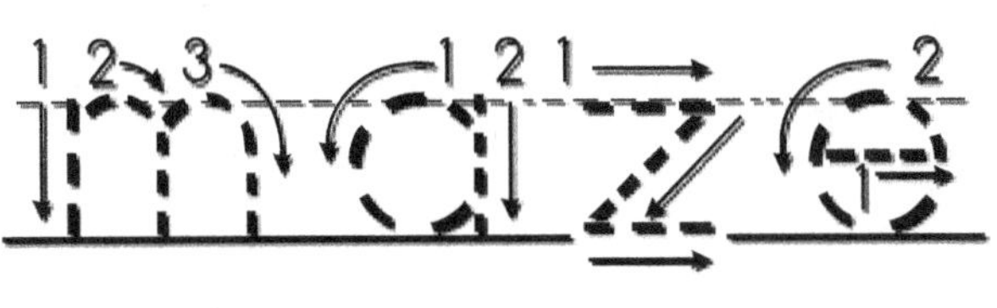

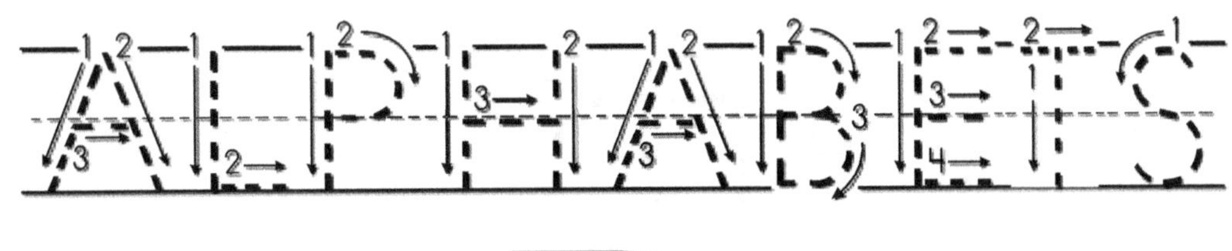

R

trace and copy the letters

R

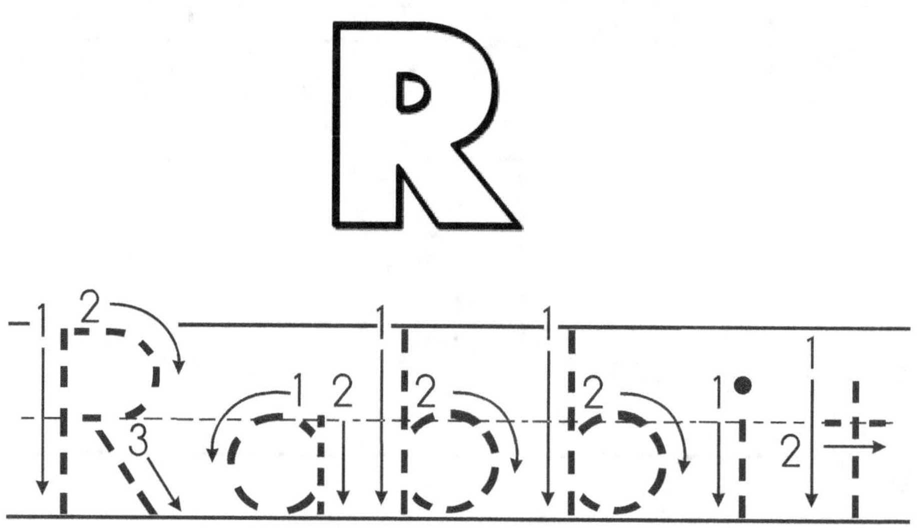

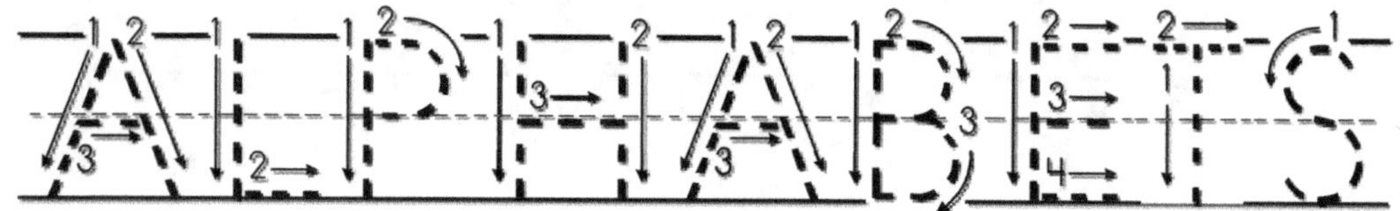

trace and copy the letters

S

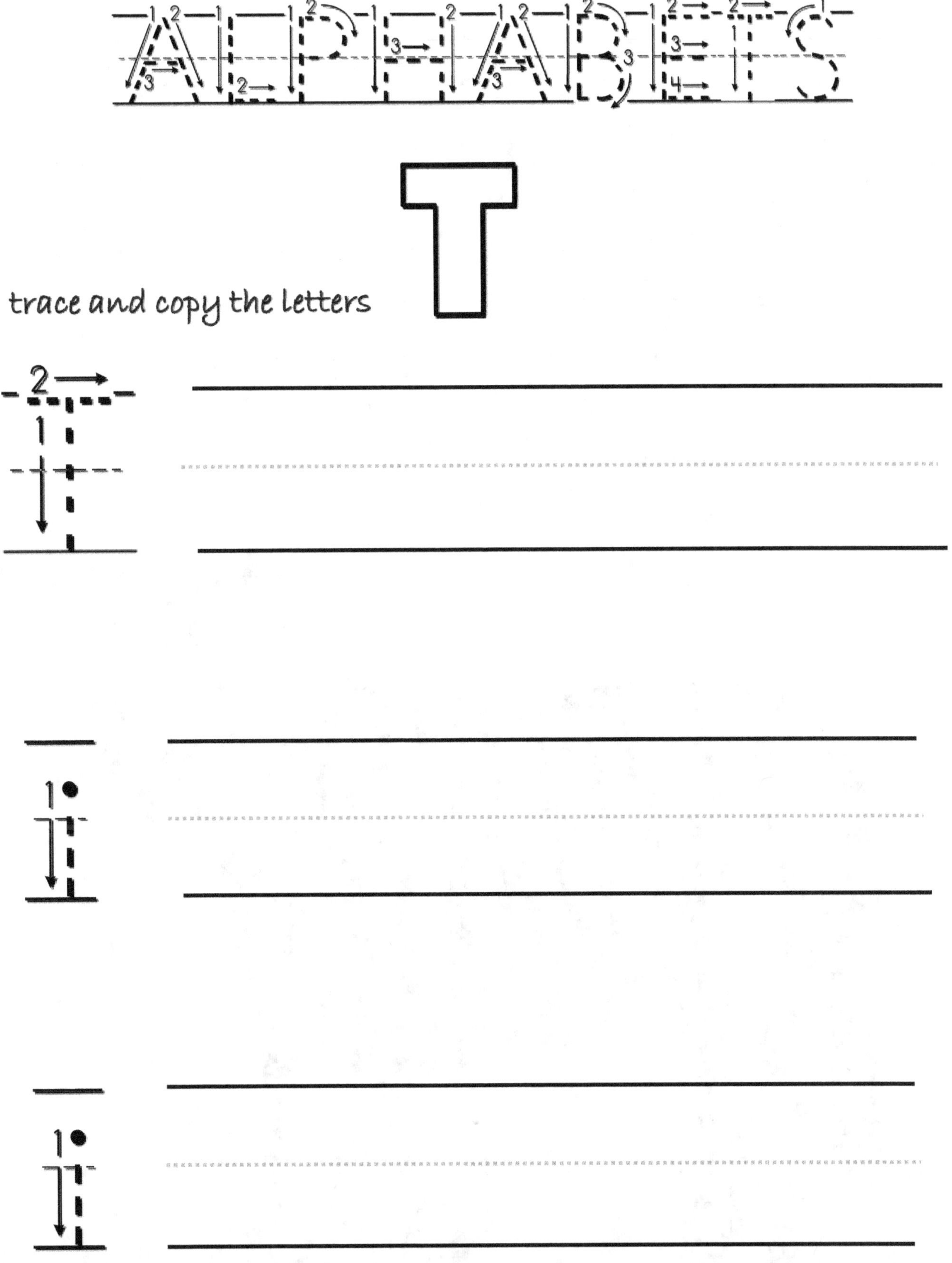

ALPHABETS

T

trace and copy the letters

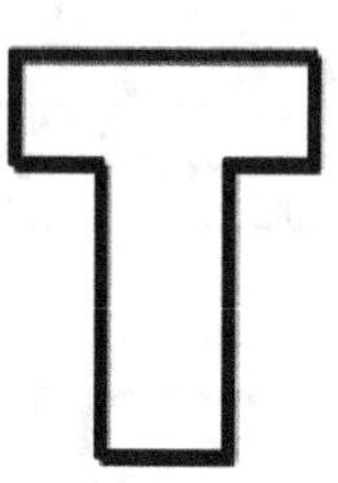

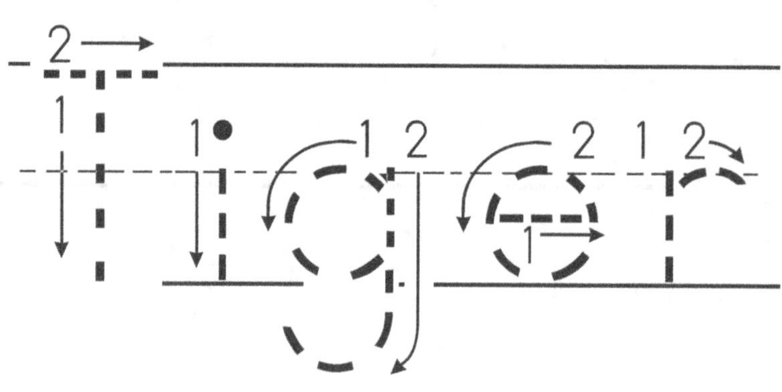

2
1
i
1 2
2 1 2
1

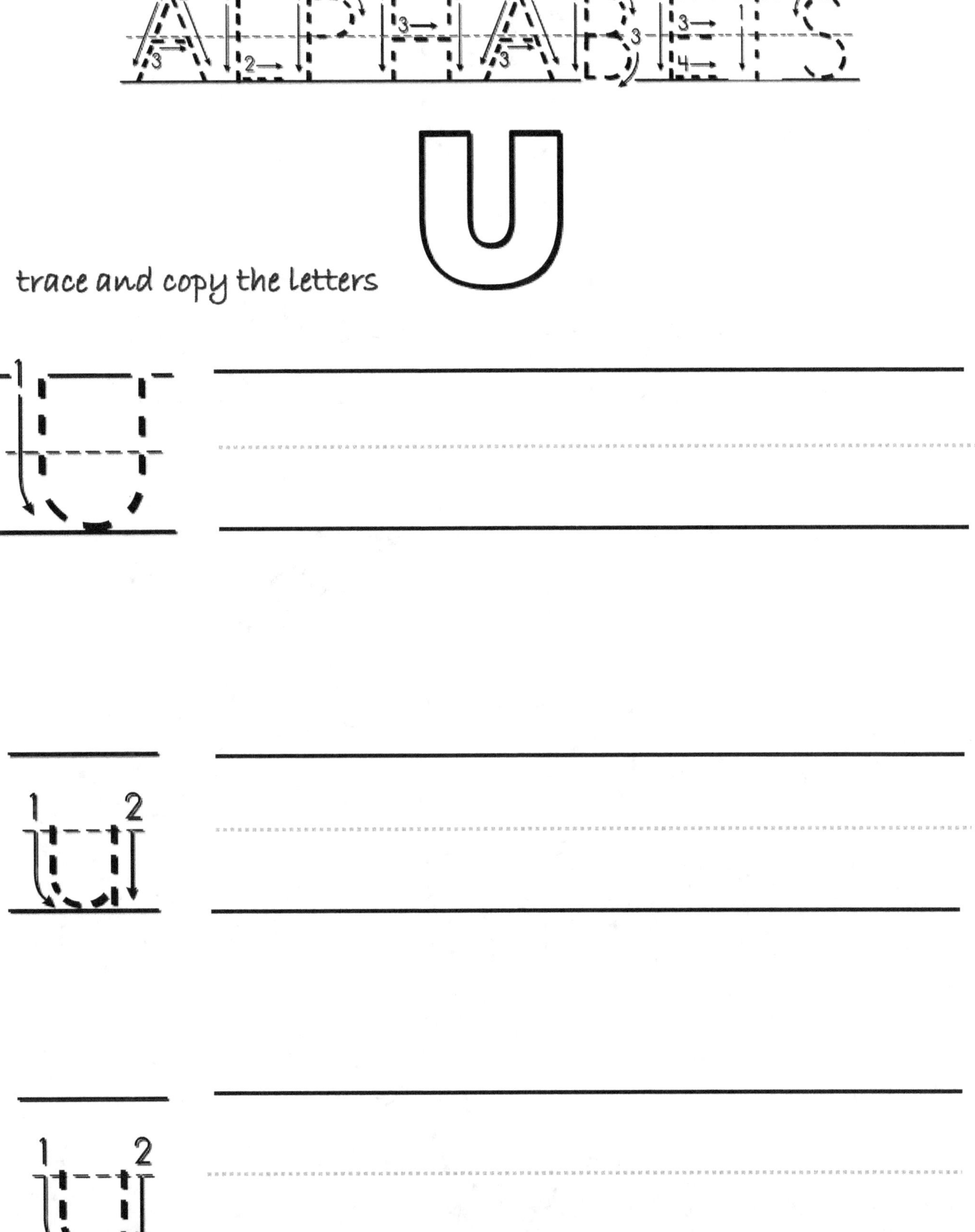

ALPHABETS

U

trace and copy the letters

U

Umbrella

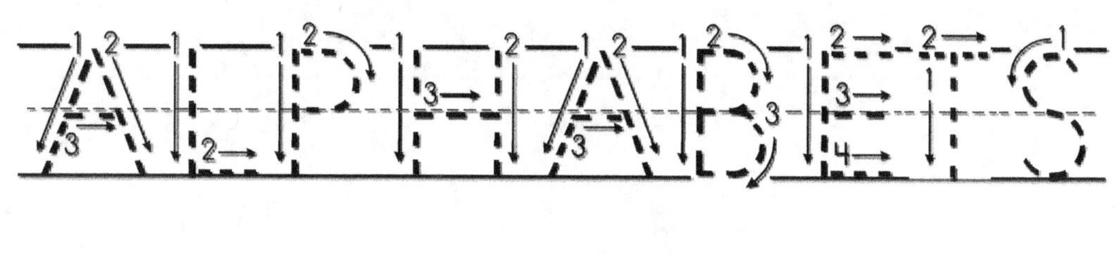

trace and copy the letters

V

Vegetables

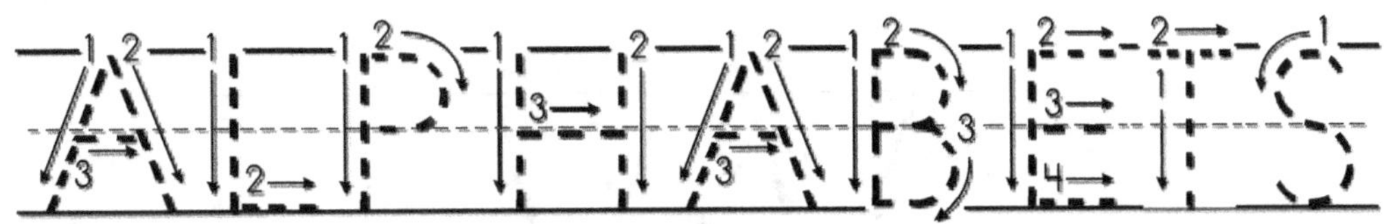

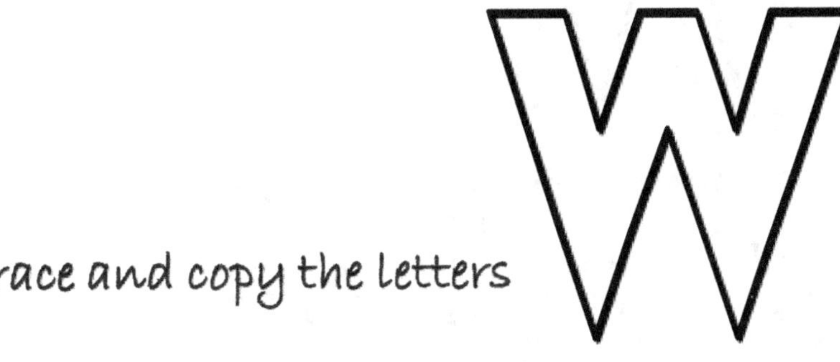

trace and copy the letters

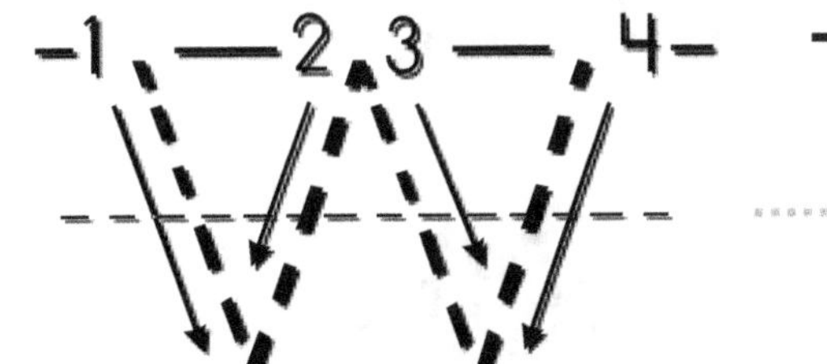

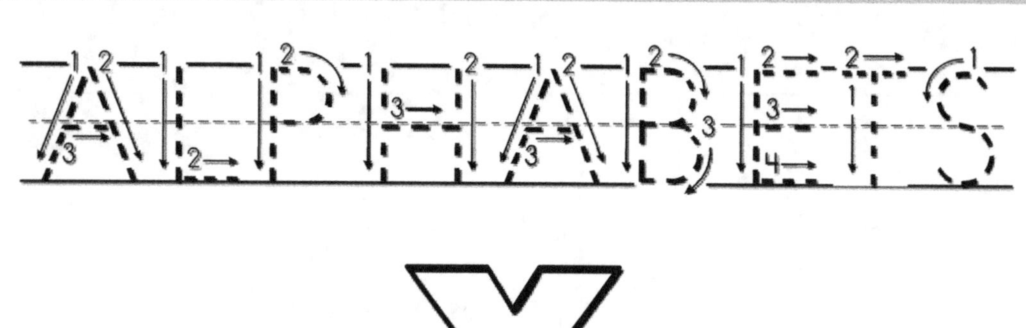

X

trace and copy the letters

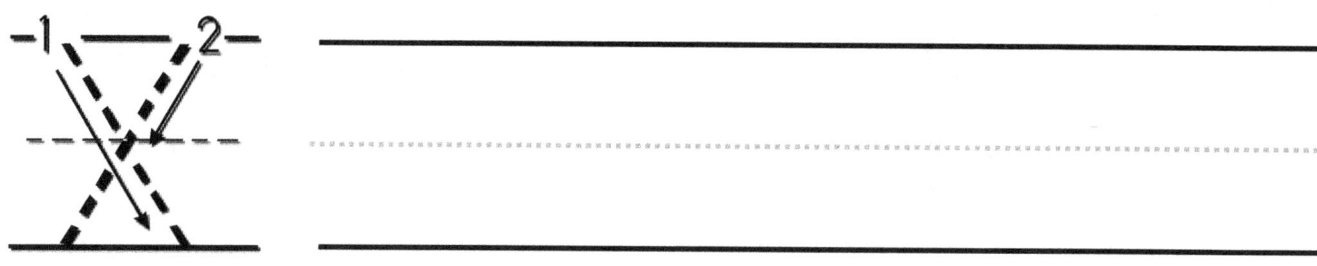

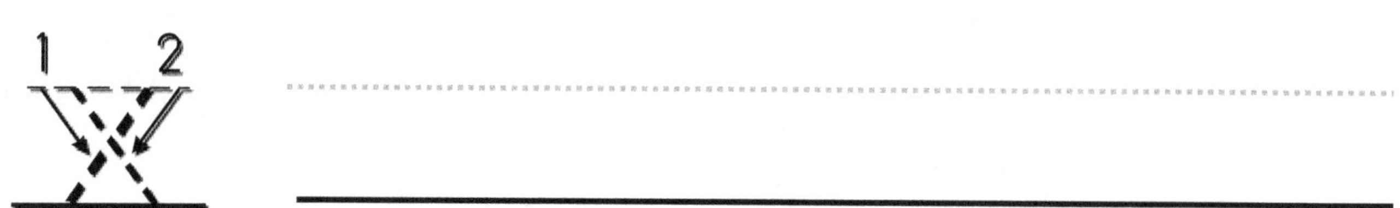

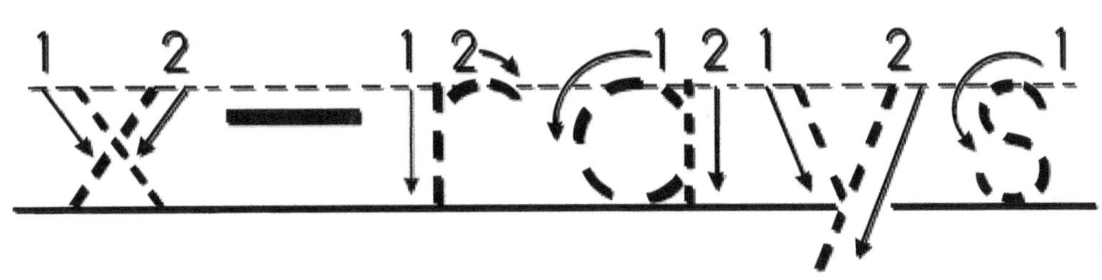

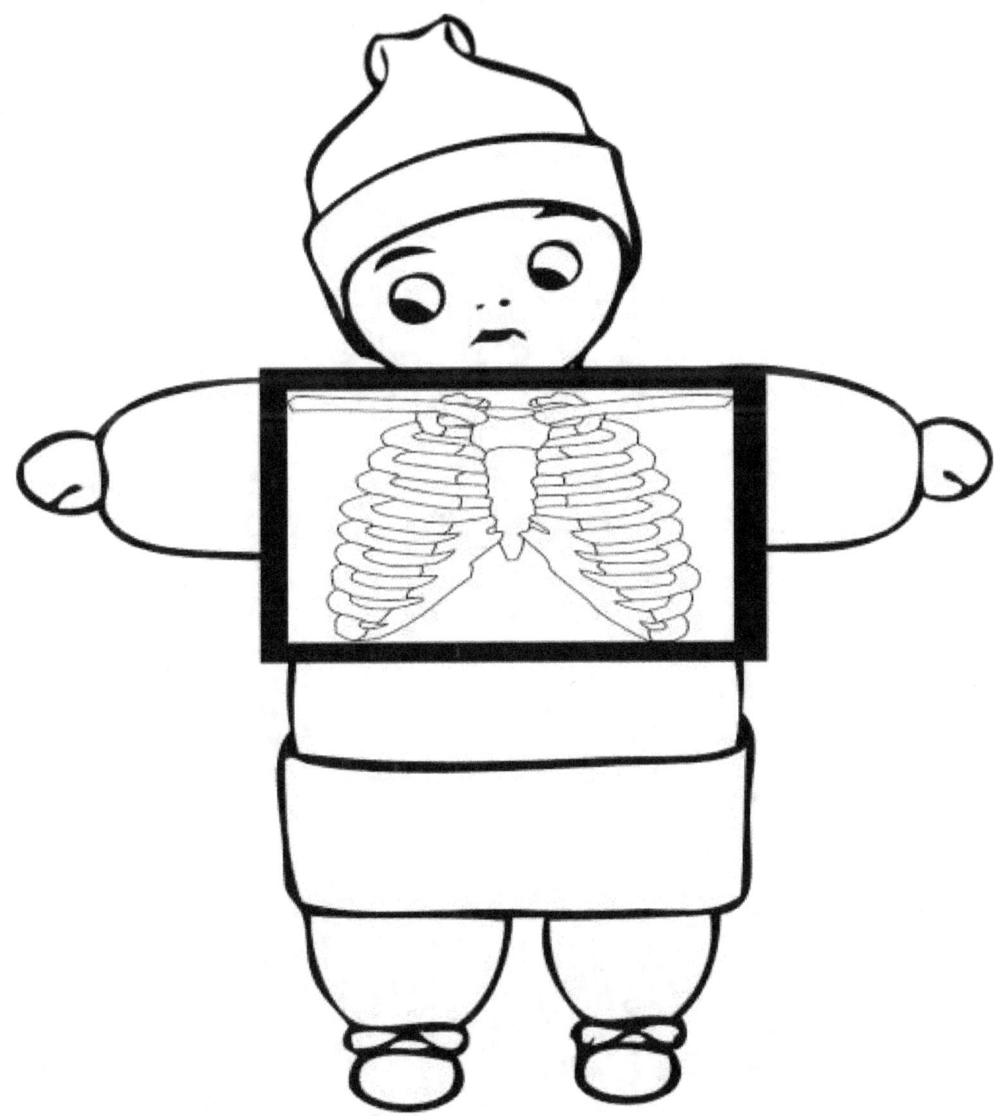

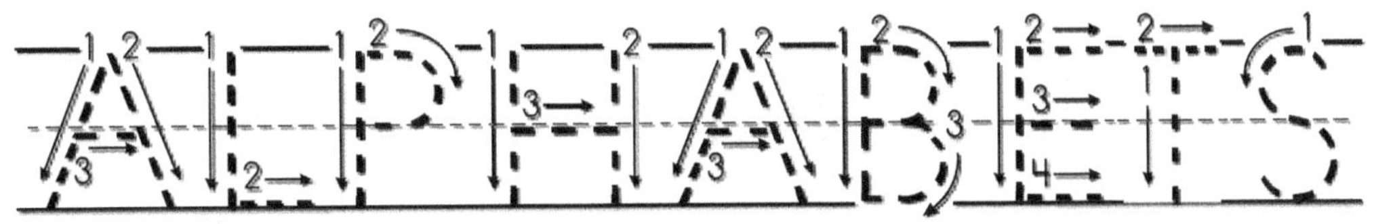

trace and copy the letters

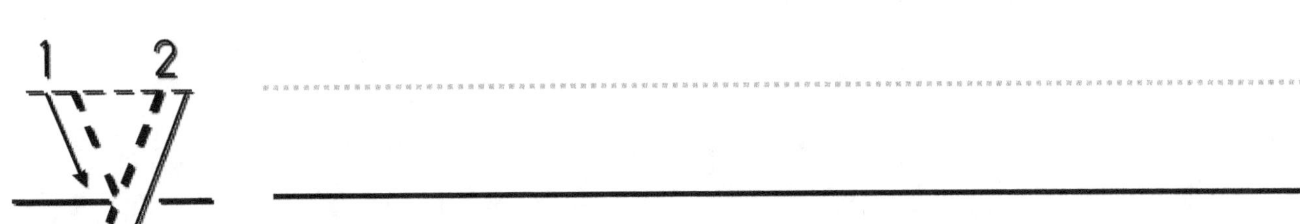

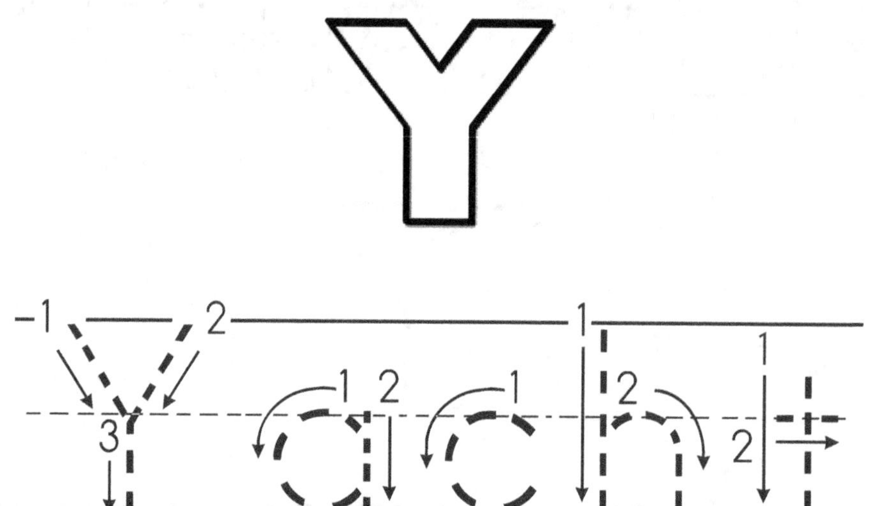

Yacht

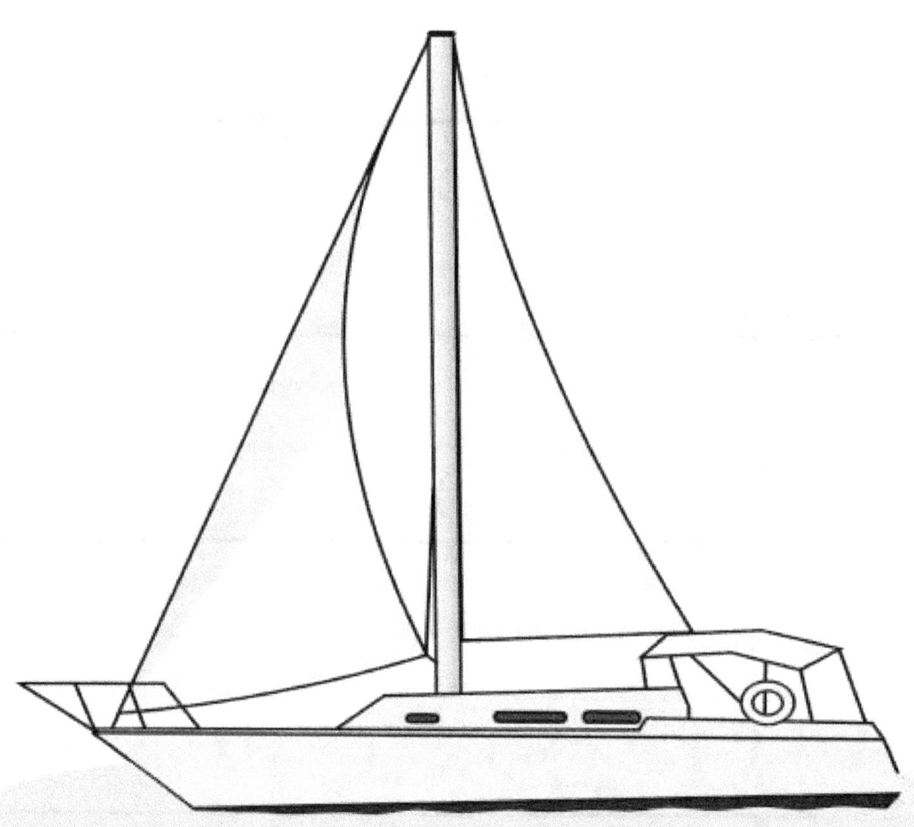

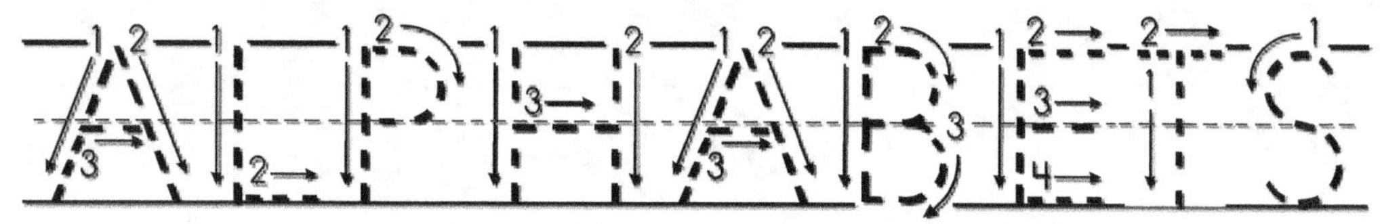

Z

trace and copy the letters

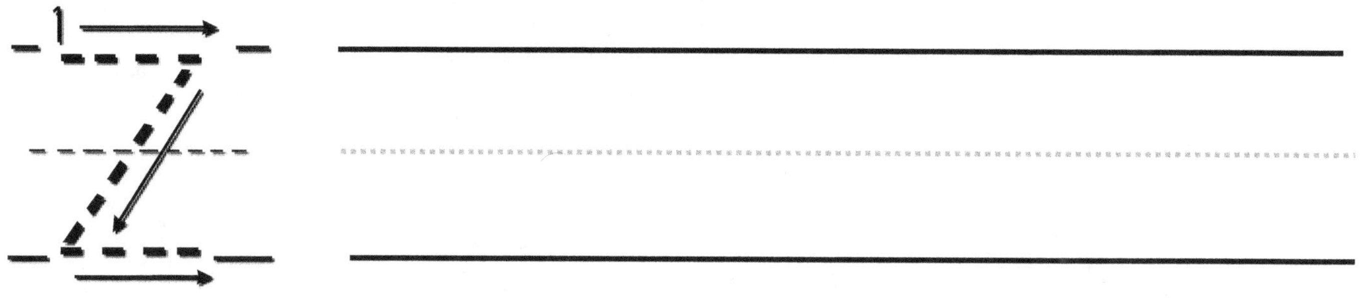

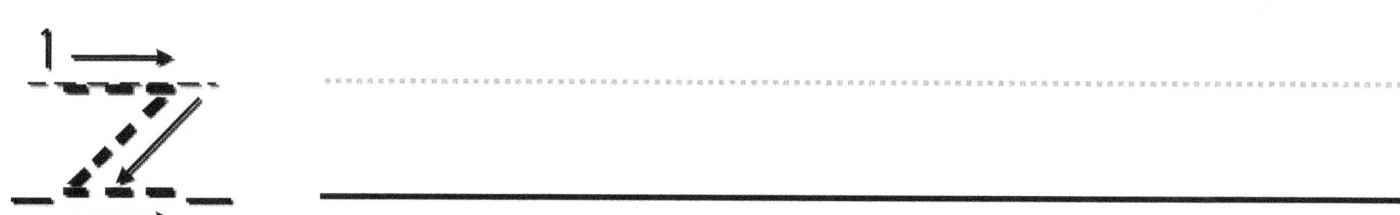

Z

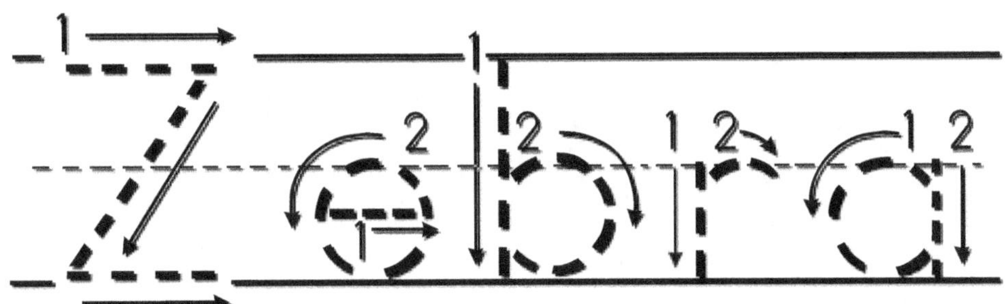